The GREATEST SPORTS STORIES NEVER TOLD

Bruce Nash and Allan Zullo ◆ **Compiled by Bernie Ward**

Illustrated by John Gampert

SIMON & SCHUSTER BOOKS FOR YOUNG READERS

Published by Simon & Schuster

New York • London • Toronto • Sydney • Tokyo • Singapore

To my daughter, Jennifer, who makes me proud to be a dad.   BN

To my mother, Alice, for all the good things she did.   AZ

To my dad. He would've loved this book.   BW

◆   ◆   ◆

Other exciting sports books by Bruce Nash and Allan Zullo

little BIG LEAGUERS™

More little BIG LEAGUERS™

little Football BIG LEAGUERS™

little Basketball BIG LEAGUERS™

Freebies for Sports Fans

ACKNOWLEDGMENTS

We wish to thank all the players, coaches, sportswriters, and researchers who helped us dig out the facts of the forgotten stories in this book.

We appreciate the assistance and cooperation of the following people: Walter Bahr, Barbara Bauer, Stanley Beals, Gary Blockus, Russell Branham, Ed Brophy, Sid Cichy, Bill Deane, Dennis Doden, Robert Driscoll, Paul Espinoza, Steve Fairchild, Mark Fickie, Gene Granger, Pat Greenleaf, Pat Harmon, Laura Hatfield, Paul Hendrickson, Hank Kaplan, Harry Keough, Marty Knack, Frank Kurth, H.J. Linford, Rita McCormick, Dick Mittman, Sam Moore, Karen Mutka, Bill Plummer III, Al Powell, Marcia Rimer, Mark Rinehiller, Mac Ruby, Pat Schmidt, Jerry Schnider, Bob Sparks, Jack Stalnaker, J. Mark Sweeney, Shirley Topley, Bruce Wigo, Larry Williams, and Tim Yonke.

Our lineup wouldn't be complete without our teammates in life, Sophie Nash and Kathy Zullo.

SIMON & SCHUSTER BOOKS FOR YOUNG READERS
Simon & Schuster Building, Rockefeller Center
1230 Avenue of the Americas, New York, New York 10020

Library of Congress Cataloging-in-Publication Data Nash, Bruce M. The greatest sports stories never told / Bruce Nash and Allan Zullo ; compiled by Bernie Ward; illustrated by John Gampert. p. cm. 1. Sports—Miscellanea—Juvenile literature. I. Zullo, Allan. II. Ward, Bernie. III. Title. GV707.N36   1993 796—dc20 92-15352 CIP AC

ISBN: 0-671-79527-9   ISBN: 0-671-75938-8 (pbk.)

CONTENTS

INTRODUCTION

The sports world is chock-full of incredible-but-true stories. Many are simply beyond belief.

Unfortunately, some of these fantastic stories have been lost over time. Newspaper accounts of remarkable sports moments get buried in the dusty libraries of halls of fame. Unbelievable events are also all but forgotten by athletes whose memories have faded over the years. And startling sports moments that happened as recently as a year ago often don't get the publicity they deserve.

While researching our sports book series, which include *little Big Leaguers* and *The Sports Hall of Shame: Young Fans' Editions,* we've uncovered loads of fantastic stories that few fans know about. We've found accounts of phenomenal feats, amazing courage, incredible incidents, and wonderful sportsmanship. So we filled this book with some of the greatest sports stories you've probably never heard of before, such as:

♦ The jockey who left the starting gate on one horse but galloped across the finish line aboard a different horse!

♦ The high school soccer game that lasted *two days!*

♦ The boxer who was knocked down a stunning 27 times—but still won!

♦ The race car that skidded across the finish line first to take the checkered flag—upside down and backward!

♦ The amazing pro baseball player who walloped a record eight home runs in one nine-inning game!

♦ The college football player who caught the game-winning touchdown pass with two broken hands!

We hope you'll be amazed and amused by the stories presented in this book. They truly are the greatest sports stories never told!

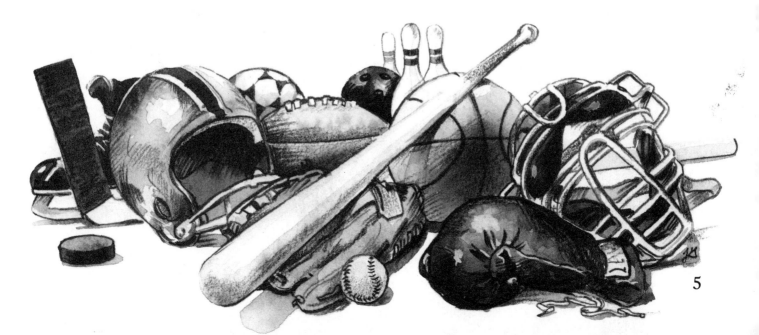

1 ♦ BLIND FAITH

On a spring afternoon in 1962, nine-year-old Billy Bradley was struck by lightning at Little League practice in El Dorado, Arkansas. He was temporarily blinded and nearly died.

The impact of that lightning bolt lasted long after Billy recovered his sight and went on to play baseball again. It forged a strong bond between the boy and his big-league idol, inspired an astonishing string of game-winning home runs, and led to an incredible twist of fate.

On April 30, 1962, Billy had just walked off the diamond with his team, the First Baptist Church, when he took a drink from the water fountain under a big oak tree next to the field. Suddenly, a deadly bolt of lightning struck the tree and hit Billy. The heat from the flash was so intense it melted Billy's cap, traveled down his right side, and exploded in the ground at his feet.

The other players and coaches were knocked to the ground and momentarily stunned. When they recovered, Billy was still unconscious, barely breathing. He was already turning blue when Coach Creed Nance reached his side. "Oh no!" cried Nance. "I think he's dead!"

Nance turned Billy on his back and started CPR. By the time help arrived, Billy was breathing again, but he remained unconscious in the hospital for two more days. When he finally regained consciousness, Billy couldn't see.

The doctors in El Dorado told Billy's parents the grim news: "The heat from the lightning badly burned his eyes. He might never see again." The boy's best hope, the doctors added, was to go to Methodist Hospital in Houston where Dr. Louis Girard was known for pioneering surgery on eye injuries. After an examination, Dr. Girard believed he could restore Billy's vision—but it would require six painful operations, three on each eye.

That same year, the Colt .45s (now called the Astros) joined the National League and started playing in Houston. Kids in El Dorado like Billy quickly adopted the Colt .45s as their team because it was the closest big-league club to their town. Billy listened to the Houston games on the radio and especially enjoyed following his favorite player, third baseman Bob Aspromonte.

When Aspromonte heard that his biggest fan was in Houston for an operation, he and some teammates went to the hospital to visit Billy. The players gave the youngster team souvenirs and a new portable radio so he could listen to the Houston games from his hospital bed.

The night before his first operation, Billy's parents took him to a Colt .45s home game. Before the contest, Billy visited his hero in the Houston locker room. Aspromonte eased Billy's nervousness about the operation and told him, "You'll see again. You must believe that. And soon you'll be playing baseball again. Now, is there anything else I can do for you?"

"Please, Bob," Billy said. "Hit a home run for me."

Aspromonte tenderly put his arm on the boy's shoulder and replied, "I'm not much of a home-run hitter. How about a bunch of base hits?"

A sad look of disappointment crossed Billy's face. "It sure would be nice if you could hit a home run."

"You're a ballplayer, so you know how hard it is to hit a homer," said Aspromonte, who averaged only five homers a year. "But I promise you, Billy, I'll try as hard as I can."

Unfortunately, Aspromonte didn't get a hit in his first three at-bats. Billy sadly returned to the hospital before the game was over because he had to get enough rest prior to the operation the next morning. So Billy listened to the final innings over his new radio from his hospital bed.

With Houston trailing the San Francisco Giants 3–1 in the bottom of the eighth inning, Aspromonte stepped up to the plate, looking for his first hit—and a chance to bring untold joy to a blind boy.

Aspromonte swung and missed badly on the first pitch. He stepped out of the batter's box and took a deep breath. For a split second, Billy's face flashed in his mind. Then the hitter got ready, determined to give the ball a ride.

Meanwhile, at the hospital, Billy pressed his ear closer to his radio and pleaded, "C'mon, Bobby, hit one for me."

The next pitch curved toward the inside of the plate, but Aspromonte was ready and whipped his bat in a sweet, powerful swing. The ball rocketed off his bat and soared high and deep toward the left-field fence.

"There's a long drive to left!" shouted the radio play-by-play man. "This could be outta here! . . . It is . . . a home run for Bob Aspromonte!"

Billy's bandaged eyes turned wet from tears of joy. "He did it!" shouted Billy. "He did it!"

Moments after the game (which Houston lost 3–2), Aspromonte was interviewed on a radio show. When he was asked about his four-bagger, he said, "This one's for you, Billy."

Those were the words that made the headlines the next morning. Before he went into surgery, Billy told his mom, "Bob Aspromonte said he'd hit a home run for me and he did. Dr. Girard said he'd make me see again and now I know he will. Bob came through for me and Dr. Girard will, too. I just know it."

The operation went as well as expected. A few days later the doctor removed the bandages. As the last bandage fell away, Billy opened his eyes for the first time since the lightning had blinded him. Billy could see light and faint shapes! His sight was coming back! But he still had a long way to go.

The next year, Billy sat out the fourth grade and was tutored at home. Soon after the 1963 baseball season opened, he went back to Houston for the second set of operations on both eyes. The surgery proved successful.

After the bandages were removed, Billy was treated to another Colt .45s game. He met his hero, Bob Aspromonte, in the Houston dugout and asked, "This time, will you hit one out that I can see?"

Aspromonte, knowing how hard it was for him to hit a homer, told Billy, "Like I told you last year, I don't know if I can, but I'll do my best—for you."

Playing against the Chicago Cubs, Aspromonte went hitless in his first four at-bats. But he got another chance in the bottom of the tenth inning with the bases loaded and one out in a 2–2 tie.

From behind the first-base dugout, Billy shouted to his idol, "C'mon, Bobby, you can do it! Smash one!"

On the very next pitch, Aspromonte belted a fastball and sent it toward the left-field wall. Billy and the 10,000 other fans in the park leaped to their feet as they followed the flight of the ball. Then they all erupted into stadium-rocking cheers as the ball landed in the outfield seats for a game-winning grand-slam home run!

As the batting hero trotted around the bases, he noticed that Billy's parents had put their son on top of the Houston dugout, leading the cheers. By the time Aspromonte touched home plate and was mobbed by his teammates, tears had welled up in his eyes. He ran to the dugout, looked up at Billy, and shouted, "That's another one for you, Billy!"

Six weeks later, Billy returned to Methodist Hospital for his third and final series of operations, which eventually fully restored the boy's sight. Just as he had done twice before, the youngster met with Aspromonte and made the same request: "Will you hit another homer for me?"

This time, Aspromonte could only shake his head and grin. "I don't hit many homers, but with you here, I really believe I'm going to hit one tonight."

Incredibly, Aspromonte came through again! In the first inning against the New York Mets, he came to bat with the bases loaded—and cracked his second grand-slam home run of the season! The round-tripper proved to be the winning margin in a 7–3 Houston victory.

"Maybe we should give that kid a con-tract," joked Colt .45s Manager Harry Craft after the game.

With his eyesight back to normal, Billy returned to the Little League diamond to play once more. He turned into a dynamite pitcher, improving with each game. Inspired by his Colt .45s hero, Billy became almost unbeatable on the mound. Three years after he was struck down by lightning, Billy pitched the greatest game of his young life. He threw a no-hitter!

A few days later, while going through his fan mail, Aspromonte opened a letter from Billy. In it was an account of the boy's pitching feat from the local El Dorado newspaper. Attached to the clipping was a note from Billy that read, "This one's for you, Bob."

But there was still one more chapter in the heartwarming story of Billy Bradley and Bob Aspromonte.

In 1974, three years after retiring from baseball, Aspromonte was working on a car battery when it exploded in his face. The battery acid blinded him.

Aspromonte underwent several eye operations to help restore part of his sight. The surgery that did the most good was nearly identical to that which Billy had— and it was performed by none other than Dr. Louis Girard, the very same surgeon who had treated the youngster!

When Billy heard about the former player's accident, he telephoned Aspromonte in the hospital. "You made me believe that I would see again," Billy told him. "I know you'll get your vision back just like I did. Don't lose faith."

Aspromonte didn't lose faith. Thanks to the surgery by Dr. Girard, 40 percent of his eyesight was restored. And now he can see again—just like Billy.

2 ◆ WHEN BABE BEAT 'EM ALL _____

The amateur track and field team known as the Golden Cyclones beat all other challengers at the combined 1932 National AAU Women's Track and Field Championship and Olympic Team Trials.

What made the performance so stunning was that the Golden Cyclones had only one athlete on the team—an 18-year-old Texas dynamo named Mildred "Babe" Didrikson.

In one incredible afternoon, the amazing one-woman team captured six gold medals and broke three world records.

Babe was already an outstanding athlete when she went to work as a typist for the Employers Casualty Insurance Company of Dallas. Although she could type 85 words a minute, her real value to the company was as the star of its amateur basketball and track and field teams, known as the Golden Cyclones.

One day, early in 1932, company official Colonel M.J. McCombs called Babe into his office and told her, "The Olympics are coming up. I want you to represent the company at the national meet and compete for a spot on the U.S. Olympic team. I've been studying the records of the other teams. I think you can do something that's never been done before—win the national team championship all by yourself."

"You know something, Colonel? I think I can, too," Babe replied confidently.

The day before the meet at Northwestern University near Chicago, Babe and Mrs. Henry Wood, the Cyclones' official chaperone, checked into a hotel. Babe tried to get some sleep, but she couldn't. The more she thought about challenging the best amateur women athletes in America all by herself, the more nervous she became.

As she tossed and turned, she felt a sharp pain in her stomach. It got so bad that a doctor was called. After examining Babe, the doctor told her, "There's nothing wrong with you other than a case of nerves. Try to relax and get some sleep."

Babe finally fell asleep just as the sun was coming up. When she awoke for the big day, Babe discovered that she had overslept! She had less than an hour to get to the stadium for her first event.

She leaped out of bed and hailed a taxi. During the long and frantic cab ride to Northwestern University, Babe hid under a blanket and changed into her track outfit. When she arrived at the campus, Babe dashed into the stadium just as the public address announcer was introducing the teams.

More than 200 women representing the best athletic clubs in the country were presented. When it came time to introduce the Golden Cyclones, a bewildered official turned to Babe and asked, "Where's the rest of your team?"

"You're looking at it," a grinning Babe replied. Then Babe sprinted out onto the

10

track by herself. She waved at the 5,000 spectators who erupted in cheers at the unexpected sight of one lone girl daring to take on the entire field of track stars.

For the next three hours, Babe dashed from one event to the other. Midway through the afternoon, Babe staggered to the sidelines during a brief break. "They've got me flying all over the place," she gasped to Mrs. Wood. "I run a heat in the 80-meter hurdles, and then take one of my high jumps. Then I have to rush over to the broad jump and right away they call me to throw the javelin or the shot put."

Mrs. Wood put a comforting arm around the sweating Babe and said, "If anybody can do it, Babe, you can."

Of the eight events she entered, Babe finished first in six of them (including one tie). She missed qualifying for the finals in the 100-meter dash and finished fourth in the discus throw.

But she wowed everyone with her first-place finishes in her other events. She heaved the 8-pound shot put 39 feet, 6¼ inches to beat Rena MacDonald, one of the best in the world. She easily outdistanced everybody in the baseball throw with a toss of 272 feet, 2 inches, and topped all competitors in the broad jump with a leap of 17 feet, 6⅝ inches.

In a preliminary heat of the 80-meter hurdles, Babe broke her own world record with an 11.9-second dash and went on to win the finals with a time of 12.1 seconds. Babe tied Jean Shiley, of Temple University, in the high jump when they both set a new world record of 5 feet, 3³⁄₁₆ inches.

The day's final event, the javelin throw, was one of Babe's strongest because she already held the world record. As she stepped to the line and gripped the javelin, Babe felt a surge of superhuman energy flow through her. She made her approach, planted her foot, hurled the spear with all her might, and watched it sail. The crowd gasped in astonishment as the javelin flew far beyond anything Babe had ever thrown before. The amazing throw was measured at 139 feet, 3 inches—nearly 6 feet farther than Babe's previous world record!

Babe finished with a team total of 30 points—8 more points than the total for the second-place Illinois Women's Athletic Club, which had a squad of 22 athletes.

As the exhausted young woman stumbled off the field at the end of the grueling meet, Mrs. Wood greeted her with a big hug. "You did it! You did it!" cried the chaperone, hugging the sweating, puffing girl. "You won the meet all by yourself!"

Just as exciting to Babe was the chance to compete in the 1932 Olympics in Los Angeles. Proving that her stunning performance at Northwestern was no fluke, a few weeks later Babe won Olympic gold medals in the high jump, 100-meter hurdles, and javelin throw.

But no one has come close to matching her achievements as a one-woman team. As one reporter who covered the meet wrote, "That was the most amazing performance ever by any individual, male or female, in track and field history!"

3 ♦ THE BUZZER BEATER

Teddy Johnson was a shy kid. He rode the bench most of the year watching his high school basketball team stumble to a dismal 4–20 season.

He would have gone pretty much unnoticed if it hadn't been for his amazing performance in a triple-overtime game against the second-ranked team in the state. Teddy came off the bench in the final 30 seconds of regulation play and tied the score with a buzzer-beating shot. Then he hit the tying basket at the buzzer of the first overtime . . . made the tying point with no time left in the second OT . . . and then in the third overtime, nailed the winning basket—again at the buzzer!

No one had ever seen such remarkable clutch shooting in high school basketball history.

Teddy and most of the guys who went out for basketball at the start of the 1971–72 season were playing together for the first time. Several small schools in the rural, southwestern Missouri hills had been consolidated into the new East Newton High in the town of Granby.

When Coach Charles Goade held the first practice of the new season, he started to mold a bunch of unknowns into a team that had to compete with other squads who had been playing together for years. He knew it would be a long season. None of the starting five was over six feet tall.

Teddy was the seventh player on the squad and occasionally filled in when one of the starters got in foul trouble. He was a quiet young man who accepted his role as a backup even though he had an amazingly accurate touch with long-range jump shots.

Teddy didn't have many opportunities to show what he could do because Coach Goade kept his starters in the lineup as much as possible, hoping to salvage a couple of victories—which were few and far between.

One of the East Newton Patriots' 20 defeats was a 60–42 thumping by the powerful Mount Vernon Mountaineers. At the time, the former state champs were ranked second and had been picked as pre-season favorites to go all the way to the Class M state finals again.

So when the two teams drew each other in the opening round of the regional tournament held at the Patriots' new gym, the Mountaineers expected another pushover in their quest for the state title. But if East Newton could whip the mighty Mountaineers, knock them out of the state tournament, and avenge its earlier loss, then the Patriots felt their first season would be a success.

Even though it had won only four games compared to 23 wins for Mount Vernon, East Newton played inspired basketball. The Patriots slowed down the pace of the game, hit a high percentage of shots, and used a strong defense to take a shocking

28–21 lead into the locker room at half-time.

But in the third period, the taller, more experienced Mountaineers outscored the Patriots 20–10 to pull ahead 41–38. However, East Newton refused to give up and stayed close throughout the fourth quarter. The Patriots trailed by just a basket, 49–47, when one of their best players, Paul Knight, fouled out with 30 seconds left in regulation play.

That's when Goade motioned to Teddy Johnson to check in. Teddy, who had never played in such a close game before, leaped off the bench. Although his heart seemed to be beating at double-time, he was surprised at how calm he felt.

Mount Vernon missed the free throw, and Goade called time-out. The coach had noticed how well Teddy was hitting his long jump shots in practice and decided to play a hunch. In the huddle, Goade said, "Teddy, see if you can get open for a last shot." Then the coach turned to his guards and ordered, "Get the ball to Teddy at the top of the key."

A surge of confidence raced through Teddy's veins when play resumed. With the fans screaming and the clock winding down, Teddy worked himself free, took the feed pass, and from 18 feet out, fired his jumper. The ball ripped through the net just as the horn sounded, ending regulation play with the score knotted at 49–all.

Teammates pounded Teddy on the back as the East Newton fans cheered wildly. "We've got 'em right where we want 'em!" shouted Knight. "Finish 'em off, Teddy!"

In the first overtime period, the Mountaineers scored two baskets, but Teddy kept the Patriots within range by drilling another long jumper. Once again, East Newton trailed by a bucket with the final seconds ticking off the clock. There was time for one more shot. Teddy got the ball at the top of the key. And like an instant replay, he drained another jumper that just beat the buzzer, tying the game again, this time 53–53.

The second overtime was such a tight defensive battle that Mount Vernon could only muster one point. Meanwhile, the Patriots were held scoreless until the final few seconds. Teddy had the ball and tried to work himself free, but was fouled a split second before the buzzer. Because it was a nonshooting foul, he had only one free throw coming.

With no time showing on the clock, Teddy stepped to the foul line. Could he save his team for a third straight time with another last-second shot? The East Newton fans held their breath while the Mount Vernon rooters yelled and whistled, hoping to upset Teddy. Despite the incredible pressure, Teddy calmly sank the free throw. He had done it again! He had rescued the Patriots from the brink of defeat and given them another chance. Now, with the score tied 54–54, the teams headed into their third OT.

During the break, Coach Goade had to shout instructions to his team over the roar of the crowd. "Teddy's got the hot hand," he yelled, pointing to the shy youngster who was suddenly the center of attention. "Let him do the shooting."

Teddy nodded. "I can make them," he said softly. "Just get me the ball."

Both teams came out firing in the third extra period. For the three baskets that the Mountaineers hit, Teddy answered with two outside jumpers and a free throw. Then, trailing 60–59 with only ten seconds left in the game, the Patriots brought the ball upcourt for one last chance to pull off the upset victory. There was no doubt who was going to try the

winning shot. Beginning with the basket that had tied the score at the end of regulation, Teddy had made all the points for East Newton.

The Mountaineers' defense kept Teddy farther away from the basket than he had hoped. They challenged him to take a long 25-foot shot that today would be from three-point range.

On the scoreboard behind the basket, Teddy saw that time was running out. Three seconds . . . He eyed the rim . . . Two seconds . . . He jumped . . . One second . . . . He fired his shot. With a flick of his wrist, he released the ball a heartbeat before the buzzer sounded.

The ball struck the rim, bounced high in the air, caromed off the backboard . . . and then fell through the basket. The Patriots had won 61–60! For the fourth time in a row, Teddy Johnson, the unlikeliest hero of all, had beaten the buzzer!

The crushed Mountaineers dropped to the floor in stunned disbelief while the joyous East Newton fans stormed the court to celebrate their astonishing victory. As Coach Goade fought his way through the pandemonium of Patriot players and fans hugging Teddy at center court, he shouted, "Unbelievable! They ought to make a movie of this—except no one would believe it!"

There was a touch of irony to Teddy Johnson's beat-the-buzzer heroics. Inspired by the win over the Mountaineers, Teddy decided to become a basketball coach. After graduating from college, Teddy's first job was as head coach of the very team he so dramatically beat—the Mount Vernon Mountaineers!

4 ◆ THE STRIKEOUT KID

Until the night of May 13, 1952, Ron Necciai was just another young, minor-league pitcher. But all that changed when the lanky, 19-year-old righthander set an astonishing record that no pitcher has ever equaled in professional baseball—he struck out 27 batters in one nine-inning game!

His amazing performance shattered the old minor-league record of 25 strikeouts and still tops the major-league mark of 20 for nine innings set by Roger Clemens of the Boston Red Sox in 1986. Necciai (pronounced NETCH-eye) pitched his sensational game for the Bristol (Tennessee) Twins against the visiting Welch (West Virginia) Miners in the Class D Appalachian League.

The Pittsburgh Pirates had signed Necciai as a first baseman in 1950. He had pitched briefly in high school in his hometown of Monongahela, Pennsylvania, but quit pitching after one of his fastballs hit a batter and broke his ribs.

However, Bristol manager George Detore convinced Necciai to pitch again. The 6-foot, 3-inch, 165-pound teenager agreed to give it another shot, but he seldom looked impressive. That's because pitching made him so nervous he developed an ulcer, which required a special diet that often left him too weak to pitch effectively.

On the night of his history-making feat, Necciai's ulcer was acting up. After warming up before the game, he told Detore, "I don't have good stuff tonight. My stomach is burning. I don't think I'll be able to pitch very long."

"Give it a try anyway, son," said the manager. "See how far you can go."

While the 1,183 fans were settling into their wooden seats at Shaw Stadium in Bristol, Necciai struck out the side in the first inning. He then retired the side in the next frame on two strikeouts and a groundout to shortstop. No one knew—or could even imagine—that the grounder would be the only fair ball hit for an out by the Miners.

In the third, Ron fanned three Miners. After returning to the dugout, Necciai told his manager, "My stomach is killing me. Maybe you should get somebody to warm up."

But Detore replied, "You're doing fine. Hang in there as long as you can." Then the manager sent the batboy to the clubhouse for some milk and cottage cheese which Ron forced down in hopes of soothing his stomach.

Over the next three innings, Necciai faced ten batters. He hit one and struck out the rest. By the start of the seventh inning, the Twins led 6–0 and Ron had chalked up 17 strikeouts.

As a joke, a Bristol fan jumped out of the stands and handed a canoe paddle with a big hole in the blade to Welch manager Jack Crosswhite, who was coaching third base. Crosswhite didn't find the joke amusing and smashed the paddle against the side of the Twins' dugout in disgust.

More Bristol fans got in the act when they began counting off the strikeouts as each Miner went down swinging. In the seventh inning, the fans chanted, "Eighteen!" . . . "Nineteen!" and then "Twenty!"

In the eighth inning, Ron called time and signaled for the batboy who raced out of the dugout with a glass of milk and a stomach pill, which the pitcher gulped down. Then the nervous pitcher struck out the side again, even though the Miners tried to bunt just to avoid striking out.

When Necciai went to the mound in the top of the ninth, he still needed two strikeouts to tie the record and three to break it. Lost in all the excitement over the whiffs was the fact that he was only three outs away from a no-hitter.

The leadoff batter hit a popup behind home plate. As catcher Harry Dunlop circled under the ball, the fans screamed, "Drop it! Drop it!" They wanted to see Necciai strike out the batter.

Dunlop deliberately let the ball fall to the ground and then caught Necciai's next pitch for strikeout number 24. With the fans screaming encouragement on each pitch, Ron fanned the next batter to tie the record. The ballpark rocked as the crowd shouted in unison, "Twenty-five!"

The teenage hurler still needed one more strikeout to do what no pro pitcher had ever done before. Necciai blew two fastballs by the batter. Then came the called third strike that put Necciai's name into the record books. But before Ron could celebrate, the ball skipped away from Dunlop and rolled back to the screen. The Miners' batter reached first on the passed ball.

But Dunlop's blunder didn't appear to bother Necciai. He struck out the last batter on three straight pitches. "Twenty-seven!" shouted the crowd as his Twins teammates rushed to the mound to congratulate Necciai on his record-smashing 7–0 no-hitter.

As if to prove the amazing, record-setting game was no fluke, Necciai's next start for Bristol was almost an instant replay—a two-hitter with 24 strikeouts.

Ron later pitched briefly in the majors. Long after Necciai hung up his glove, the National Association of Professional Baseball Leagues voted on the 50 most famous minor-league records. Ron Necciai's incredible strikeout performance was listed as number one.

5 ♦ INDY'S BEST-KEPT SECRET

When race car driver Chet Miller went in for a pit stop halfway through the 1930 Indianapolis 500, officials refused to let him continue until a broken spring was fixed. Unfortunately, Miller didn't have the spare part.

But that didn't stop Miller and his crew. The quick-thinking men rushed into the infield where many Indy fans had parked their cars. There, the crew removed a spring from an auto, installed it in Miller's racer, and watched him roar back onto the track!

Miller finished in the money—and then returned the borrowed spring without the car owner ever knowing about it!

Days before the Indy 500, Miller, a 24-year-old race car driver from Detroit, was admiring his car, known as a Fronty-Ford. The sleek black-and-green racing machine had performed better than expected during the qualifying rounds with an average speed of 97.36 MPH, which was pretty fast for those days.

"I have a feeling this baby is going to win," Miller told his mechanics. "Everything looks great. Now, are you sure we have all the extra parts we'll need for the race?"

His chief mechanic, Jim Prock, nodded

and replied with a joke, "As long as you don't total the car."

Dreaming about winning the $50,000 first prize, Miller broke out in a big grin and said, "I can almost see myself getting the checkered flag and then rolling in the dough." Then his expression changed into a frown. "I just hope I don't get fouled up by some small little problem."

"Don't worry," said Prock. "The boys and I will find a way to fix anything that goes wrong."

On the day of the race, a record-breaking crowd of 170,000 jammed the Indianapolis Speedway. Cars from all over the country were parked in the infield and for miles around outside the track.

"I have a feeling this day is going to be a day I'll never forget," said Miller as he climbed into his Fronty-Ford. He was right about his feeling, but not in a way he could ever have imagined.

Thirty-eight race cars lined up for the start. Then, with a cloud of smoke and a roar of engines, the race got underway around the famous 2½-mile brick oval. Everything was running smoothly for Miller's Fronty-Ford as he worked his way through the pack. After the first 50 laps of the 200-lap race, Miller was within striking distance of the leaders. He was averaging close to 100 MPH and still felt good about his chances of winning.

But then he came across a spectacular six-car pileup. As Miller weaved his way through the wreckage, his car broke one of its front springs. Despite the problem, Miller continued in the race and went in for a pit stop after the 92nd lap to have the carburetor adjusted.

But when race officials examined his Fronty-Ford, they saw the broken front spring and refused to let Miller back in the race until it was replaced.

Angry and frustrated by the bad break, Miller turned to his crew and barked, "Get it fixed . . . and fast!"

"We can't," said one of the mechanics. "We don't have an extra spring."

"Well, then, find one!"

Suddenly, Prock came up with a brainstorm. "If we can take one off of someone else's Ford," he told Miller, "I should be able to make it work in your car."

Miller, Prock, and the crew then dashed into the infield and began searching for the right kind of Ford. It took only a few minutes to find one. But there was no owner in sight to get permission to use the spring.

"We can't afford to waste any more time," Miller told Prock. "Just take the spring out now."

"That's stealing," said Prock.

"No," Miller replied. "That's borrowing. We'll put it back after the race."

So Prock slipped under the Ford, took off the front spring, raced back to Miller's car, and installed it to the satisfaction of the race officials. Forty-one minutes after he had first pulled in for a pit stop, Miller was back in the race.

Although his dreams of winning were gone, he still drove as hard as he could and finished in 13th place—one of only 14 drivers who completed the race. Miller, who won $400, stepped out of the Fronty-Ford and thanked his men. "You did a fine job," he told them. "I think I would've had a shot at winning if it hadn't been for that darn spring."

"The spring!" shouted Prock. "We better get it back before the owner finds out or drives away without it." Prock raced over to the Ford, reinstalled the spring, and left before the owner returned.

The owner never did find out that a piece of his car helped a driver finish the Indianapolis 500.

6 ◆ THE 'OLD MAN' IN THE NET

In the second game of the 1928 Stanley Cup finals, the New York Rangers were in trouble. Their only goalie had just been carried off the ice with a serious injury and they needed a replacement. But none of the Rangers had played that position. Coach Lester Patrick had to do something.

Even though he hadn't skated in a game in three years, Patrick suited up, went into the net—and became the hero of the game!

The Rangers had entered the best-of-five championship as the underdog and promptly lost the first game 2–0 to the Montreal Maroons.

For the second contest, more than 14,000 rowdy fans were on hand at the Montreal Forum, rooting for another Maroon victory. The first period was scoreless. Then, minutes into the second period, disaster struck the Rangers. A puck fired by Montreal center Nels Stewart, the leading scorer of his day, smashed into the left eye of Rangers goalie Lorne Chabot, knocking him out. The crowd fell silent as the injured Ranger was carried off the ice on a stretcher.

At the time, there was no such thing as a second-string goalie. The referees told Patrick he had ten minutes to get a replacement or the match would be forfeited to the Maroons.

Alex Connell, the goalie for the Ottawa Senators, was watching the game and he came out of the stands to volunteer his services. However, before using Connell, Patrick had to get permission from Maroons coach Eddie Gerard. But Gerard flatly rejected the request.

Patrick stared at his rival in stunned disbelief. "Wait a minute, Eddie," he said. "Aren't you forgetting something? What about 1922? You remember what I did for you."

In the 1922 Stanley Cup play-offs, the men were involved in a similar situation, only reversed. That year, Patrick was coaching Vancouver against Toronto. When the Toronto goalie went down with an injury, Patrick graciously allowed the opposing team to use an emergency replacement. That substitute was none other than Eddie Gerard. He starred in two Toronto victories, costing Vancouver the Stanley Cup.

Now, when it came time for him to repay the favor, Gerard turned his back on Patrick. "Suckers like you were born yesterday," Gerard told him. "You're talking to the wrong guy. If I let you use Connell, it could cost me the game. I can't hear you."

Coaches from other hockey teams, who were watching the game, pleaded with Gerard to be fair and let Patrick use Connell. Gerard still refused. By then, the news of his refusal had reached the crowd. Nearly all of the fans were Maroon supporters, but in a wink they turned on

the Montreal coach, howling in anger over his lack of sportsmanship.

Meanwhile, Patrick was running out of time and he didn't know what to do. But then Rangers center Frank Boucher asked, "Why don't you play goal?"

"No, I'm too old," the 45-year-old coach replied. "I haven't skated in a game in three years." But the other Rangers urged him to try. Reluctantly, Patrick agreed to suit up. After putting on Chabot's equipment, skates, and jersey—which all fit perfectly—the silver-haired coach shakily skated onto the ice. His dramatic appearance was met with a roaring standing ovation as the Montreal fans switched their allegiance to cheer for the gutsy, over-the-hill Rangers coach.

As they skated out for the face-off, the Maroons didn't bother to conceal their glee. "Hey, old man," shouted Montreal's Hooly Smith. "We're going to run you right off the ice."

"Just try," growled Boucher. "You lay a stick on him and you answer to me."

When the game resumed, the Maroons launched a quick, aggressive attack on the substitute goalie. But Patrick played like an all-star in his prime, blocking shot after shot. He skated behind the net to break up plays, dove headlong onto the ice to foil Montreal's blistering shots, and fought off the younger, stronger Maroons who tried to muscle him out of the net.

Inspired by their coach's sensational effort, the Rangers caught fire. They became fiercely protective of their courageous coach and flattened any Maroon who got too close to Patrick. Then, early in the third period, the Rangers scored the first goal of the game.

The valiant New York goalie continued to stop shot after shot. But with six minutes left to play, the Maroons finally slapped a goal past him to tie the score 1–1 and eventually send the game into sudden death overtime.

The Maroons were frustrated by their inability to beat Patrick and they were angered that their fans were cheering his every move. So the team launched a ferocious attack, bombarding the goalie with vicious slap shots. But the brave substitute blocked every one.

Then, when Patrick felt he was about to collapse from exhaustion, it was all over. The Rangers' Ching Johnson picked up a loose puck and charged toward the Maroons' net. At the last second, he passed off to Boucher, who slammed the puck into the net for the game-winning goal!

Pandemonium erupted around the Rangers' net as Patrick slumped to his knees in joy. He was instantly surrounded by his happy teammates who hoisted the player-coach onto their shoulders and carried him off the ice in triumph.

When New York's regular goalie, Chabot, returned to action, the inspired Rangers won two of the next three games to capture the Stanley Cup. The first thing the victorious players did when they received their prized trophy was hand it to their coach-turned-goalie-turned-hero—Lester Patrick.

7 ◆ JAMES THORNTON'S WILD RIDE

In one of the craziest races of all time, jockey James Thornton left the starting gate on one horse but galloped across the finish line aboard a different horse!

It was the only time a jockey ever switched horses in the middle of a race. And he didn't even realize he did it until after the race was over!

Thornton, a jockey for 12 years, was one of the few black riders on the racing circuit in 1970. But his friendship with fellow veteran jockey Danny Gallegos, a white, helped Thornton find acceptance among the other jockeys. In the jockeys' room before and after races, Thornton and Gallegos played card games, shared meals, and often helped each other get ready for a race.

Neither could imagine what was about to happen to them on a rainy night at the muddy Charles Town (West Virginia) Race Track on June 25, 1970.

Both jockeys changed into clean silks for the ninth race and went to the paddock to mount up. Gallegos climbed aboard Kandi Arm, a big sorrel with a nervous temperament that pranced from side to side. Gallegos patted Kandi Arm's neck and spoke soothingly to calm him down as the horses and riders moved into the starting gate.

A couple of stalls over, Thornton was atop Native Bird, a dark chestnut and one of the favorites in the race since the horse usually ran good in mud. An instant later, the starter's bell rang, the gate sprang open and they were off.

It was a close race from start to finish, but Thornton and Gallegos were not among the leaders. The two were stuck in the middle of the pack right next to each other. As their two big thoroughbreds thundered down the backstretch side by side, they were so close that sparks flew when the jockeys' stirrups banged against each other.

Suddenly, the unbelievable happened. As Thornton raised his whip to urge on Native Bird, he accidentally struck Kandi Arm across the nose, one of a horse's most sensitive areas. Kandi Arm was so startled by getting whacked that he banged into Native Bird.

The impact sent Gallegos flying backward over Kandi Arm's rear and tumbling onto the track. Fortunately, the muddy surface broke his fall and he walked away with only minor bruises.

But Thornton's wild ride was just beginning. The collision tossed Thornton straight up in the air. As he came down between the two horses, he desperately grabbed at a handful of mane and wound up under the horse's neck. Hanging onto the mane for dear life, the jockey managed to pull himself up on the back of the thoroughbred, and swing into the saddle. Then he retrieved the dangling reins and brought the mount under control.

Despite his close brush with disaster,

the mud-caked Thornton still finished the race in sixth place. He breathed a sigh of relief and reached down to pat his horse. Only then did the jockey notice with amazement that he was aboard a mount wearing number 5. The horse he had started on was number 3!

Kandi Arm's trainer, Bob Arnett, rushed to his side as Thornton slid shakily to the ground.

"Are you OK, Danny?" shouted Arnett anxiously. "That was some collision! Is James hurt?"

"I'm James," answered Thornton. He pointed to the track. "Danny is still out there somewhere."

The bewildered trainer stepped closer. He scraped a layer of gooey mud off Thornton's face, peered closely, and exclaimed, "My goodness! I sent a white jockey out on my horse and a black one came back!"

Just then, Danny Gallegos trudged in from the muddy track, limping slightly. The two jockeys stared at each other, both stunned by their incredible ordeal.

Thornton threw his arm around his friend's shoulder. "Man," he said. "I'm sure glad you're OK."

Gallegos returned the embrace and said, "I'm sure glad you're OK—and brought my horse home!"

24

8 ◆ THE KING OF CLOUT

On a hot, dusty Sunday afternoon in Ennis, Texas, Jay Justin "Nig" Clarke stepped to the plate in the bottom of the first inning of a minor-league game and knocked the very first pitch thrown to him over the right-field fence for a home run.

The four-bagger signaled the beginning of a record-setting batting feat which has never been equaled. By the end of the day, on June 15, 1902, Clarke had put his name in the history books. He went to the plate eight times—and blasted eight home runs! Not even great sluggers like Babe Ruth or Hank Aaron hit that many in one game. In fact, only nine major leaguers have smacked four homers in one contest.

At the time of his incredible home-run barrage, Clarke was a 19-year-old, switch-hitting catcher from Ontario, Canada, playing in his first season of organized baseball. The stocky, 5-foot, 8-inch rookie swung a mean bat and was one of the big reasons his team, the Corsicana Oilers, was riding a red-hot, 27-game winning streak in the old Texas League.

The game between the first-place Oilers and the last-place Texarkana Cowboys was originally scheduled to be played in Corsicana. But a town law prohibited the minor leaguers from playing baseball on Sundays, so the game was moved 20 miles away to nearby Ennis, Texas.

Clarke was anxious to bat, especially when he saw who was pitching. Texarkana hurler John DeWitt, an 18-year-old rookie, was on the mound only because his father owned the team and ordered the manager to let his boy pitch.

Reluctantly, the Texarkana manager started DeWitt. The greenhorn pitcher promptly gave up six runs in the first inning, including Clarke's first round-tripper of the day. To embarrass the owner, the skipper left the weak-armed hurler in for the whole game—a game that turned into a batting practice session for the happy Oilers.

In the bottom of the third inning, trailing 8–1, DeWitt faced Clarke for the second time. Once again, Clarke whacked the ball out of the park. The pitcher gave up so many runs in the inning that Clarke batted for a second time in the frame and clouted his third four-bagger of the day.

In the fifth inning, with Corsicana winning 25–1, Clarke belted his fourth homer to the glee of the Oiler fans who had followed the team to Ennis. They cheered his every trip to the plate, begging for more home runs.

When Clarke rounded the bases after his fourth homer, a wealthy cattleman jumped out of the stands and met the slugger as he crossed the plate. "Here, son," said the rancher. "You earned this." He then handed the shocked ballplayer a $50 bill as a reward.

A rival cattleman didn't want to be out-

Texas wind sprang up, blowing from home plate out to right field. On his last two at-bats, Clarke managed to hit the ball high enough for the wind to carry it over the fence in right.

Teammate Tommy Morris was waiting at home to shake Clarke's hand for the eighth straight time that afternoon. "Don't tell anybody," a grinning Clarke whispered to Morris, "but that last one just barely got over."

When the slugfest finally ended, the cheering Corsicana fans collected an additional $85 to show their appreciation for Clarke's astounding feat. Along with the $105 in bonuses from the two rich cattlemen, the $190 was more than the stunned player made in a month.

"I'm going back home and buy enough shoes and shirts to last a year," Clarke told his admiring fans.

Clarke's team won the game by the lopsided margin of 51–3! Some telegraph operators who relayed baseball scores to local newspapers were so convinced there was a typographical error that they changed the score to read 5–3.

The Oilers scored at least twice in every inning, pounded out 53 hits, and clubbed 21 homers as two of Clarke's teammates walloped three homers apiece.

Clarke's historic batting performance attracted big-league scouts. Before long, he moved up to the majors and stayed there for nine years, playing 506 games for the Cleveland Indians, Detroit Tigers, St. Louis Browns, Philadelphia Phillies, and Pittsburgh Pirates.

But Nig Clarke never displayed any real power in the bigs. In fact, he had only six round-trippers during his entire major-league career!

done. When Clarke trotted off the field following his fifth round-tripper in a row, the cattleman was waiting at the dugout with another bonus—this time $55.

In the dugout after his sixth homer, the slugger nudged teammate Mike O'Connor, pointed to the hapless DeWitt on the mound, and said, "I'm sure glad that kid can't pitch. He's been feeding me stuff all day."

Although most of Clarke's homers were long pokes, he did have a little help from Mother Nature in the late innings. A brisk

9 ♦ THE SUCKER PUNCH

Boxer Kid McCoy beat world welterweight champion Tommy Ryan by tricking the title holder out of his crown.

Until the Kid came along, Ryan was known in boxing circles as one of the smartest fighters around. During an amazing career that lasted 20 years, Ryan won 68 bouts by knockouts. In all those fights, Ryan was kayoed only one time—by Kid McCoy.

The Kid, whose real name was Norman Selby, learned to box as a youngster in Indiana. He was 17 years old when he first saw Ryan fight in a match against Con Doyle in 1890. Although Doyle was a strong welterweight, Ryan knocked him out in the 28th round.

The fight left an enormous impression on McCoy, who was beginning to make a local name for himself as a young, cocky amateur boxer. The Kid marveled at how easily Ryan danced around the ring, flicking jabs at the bewildered Doyle. "That," McCoy told a friend, "is what I'm going to be. Only better. You wait and see. I'll be the champion before you know it."

A year after that bout, the Kid tracked down Ryan at the fighter's home training camp near Redwoods, New York. "Mr. Ryan," announced McCoy, "I'm a pretty good boxer myself. How about taking me on as a sparring partner?"

Ryan looked at the lean, 160-pound, 5-foot, 11-inch, well-built teenager and agreed to hire him as his sparring partner.

But, just to be mean, Ryan knocked the stuffing out of the green youngster every time they got into the ring. In those days, most boxers fought a dozen or more bouts a year, so McCoy spent a lot of time being a human punching bag while Ryan prepared for his fights.

But while Ryan was happily knocking him around the ring, the Kid was learning all of Ryan's moves, strategies, and punches. He studied Ryan's boxing style—and swore that someday he'd use that knowledge to get even.

For his plan to work, McCoy didn't want Ryan to know just how good he was. Through constant practice, the Kid learned how to move backward and sideways as fast as most other fighters could move forward.

He also discovered that Ryan, like many boxers of the day, was a sucker for a left-handed punch. So McCoy worked hard on using his left hand as naturally as he used his right. He secretly ate, wrote, and threw baseballs with his left hand. That way, when he got into the ring, he was armed with a left-handed punch that no one expected.

But he kept all his skills a secret. When he sparred with Ryan, the Kid often cringed and pretended he was afraid. Once he begged Ryan not to punch him on the chest. "Please don't hit me around the heart," he pleaded. "It hurts and makes me sick. If I didn't need the money,

I wouldn't even be fighting." Since Ryan was a bully, he kept on pounding McCoy. That was fine with the Kid because he wanted Ryan to believe that he (McCoy) was a weakling who couldn't stand up to a real fighter.

McCoy soon felt he was ready to go out on his own. In 1893, at the age of 20, the Kid won 12 bouts, 9 by knockout in his first full year as a professional.

Meanwhile, Ryan continued to win. In 1894, he became the welterweight champion of the world when he beat Mysterious Billy Smith in a decision. After that, Ryan waltzed through several more easy fights. However, the lack of serious competition made him flabby and lazy.

McCoy realized that now was the time to challenge the champ. But every time the Kid asked for a fight, Ryan turned him down. "This guy ain't no fighter," Ryan snorted to his manager. "I'm not going to waste my time on him."

The only way the Kid got the chance to box Ryan was by tricking the champ into a match. McCoy dusted white powder on his face to make himself look sickly. Then—stooped over, coughing, and clutching at his chest—the Kid managed to bump into Ryan on the street. The champ was shocked by the pitiful appearance of his former sparring partner.

"I'm a sick man, Tommy," coughed the Kid. "The doctor says I got consumption [a form of tuberculosis] and may not last another year. Please give me a fight. I need the money to pay my doctor bills and to leave a few dollars for my starving family."

Although Ryan was a bully, he felt sorry for McCoy and agreed to a match. When Ryan disappeared around the corner, the Kid straightened up, wiped the powder off his face, and danced down the street. His trick had worked perfectly! The unsuspecting Ryan had been suckered into granting the "dying" boxer a title fight.

During the weeks leading up to the fight, McCoy trained as hard as ever while Ryan loafed. The champ was confident that he could knock out the frail Kid with one punch.

The bout was held March 2, 1896, at the Empire Athletic Club in Maspeth, New York. When the two fighters climbed through the ropes, Ryan received a shock. Instead of the sick opponent he expected, Ryan faced a snarling, powerful—and very healthy—Kid McCoy.

Out of shape and slow, Ryan threw weak punches in the early rounds that McCoy easily danced away from. The Kid threw sharp jabs and stinging punches that soon had the champion stumbling around the ring in a daze. In the fifth and sixth rounds, McCoy decked Ryan, but both times the bell saved the desperate champ. In the ninth round, the Kid again floored Ryan.

Then in the 15th round, McCoy finished off the champ with a powerful left-handed punch to the chin. This time when Ryan went down, he stayed down as the referee counted him out—for the first and only time in his long career. Kid McCoy was the new welterweight champion of the world!

After he was revived, Ryan staggered across the ring and grudgingly congratulated the new champion. "But you tricked me," Ryan complained. "You're not the sick man I met on the street corner."

Kid McCoy spread his arms wide, grinned, and said, "You're right, Tommy. What you see here today is the real McCoy!"

10 ♦ THE INVISIBLE PITCH

Seventeen-year-old pitcher Dennis Overby signed a minor-league contract fresh out of high school because he could throw a nasty knuckleball.

However, he won his first professional game thanks in part to throwing an imaginary baseball!

As the star of his high school team in Chetek, Wisconsin, the left-handed hurler attracted the attention of big-league scouts. Right after graduation in the spring of 1959, the Milwaukee Braves signed the youngster to a contract that included a $100,000 bonus. Overby then joined the McCook (Nebraska) Braves in the Class D Rookie League.

But in his first start for McCook, Overby was pounded for 14 runs in 6 innings. He never made it past the second inning in his next two starts. So manager Bill Steinecke told the disappointed rookie, "You're going to be working out of the bullpen from now on."

Overby, crushed by the demotion, wondered if he would ever get another chance to start a game. While feeling sorry for himself, he soon discovered that there were some benefits to being so far away from the action on the field. The bullpen crew could goof off—and get away with it. The bullpen at McCook Stadium was out in the far corner of left field where the dim lights of the ancient ballpark barely penetrated the gloom. To Steinecke and the players in the dugout, the bullpen crew were only obscure figures way out in the shadows.

Overby learned that the best thing about being stuck in the bullpen was the food he could eat during the game—even though it was against the rules. Relief pitchers often convinced fans in the bleachers to buy them goodies to eat in exchange for bullpen baseballs.

One steamy night when the Braves were playing a home game against the Holdrege White Sox, Overby got hungry because he had missed dinner. So he offered a fan a baseball in exchange for a hot dog and soft drink.

"Tell you what," said the fan. "Make it two balls and I'll get you some french fries, too."

"It's a deal," said Overby. Only after he sneakily ate his meal did the hurler realize that there was only one ball left in the bullpen for pitchers to use for warming up.

In the top of the ninth inning, Overby again was attacked by hunger pains. With a new relief pitcher in the game and the Braves holding a comfortable 11–5 lead, Overby gave in to temptation and traded away the last ball in the bullpen for another hot dog and soda.

Just as he swallowed his last bite, the White Sox erupted for four runs. Steinecke then sent the batboy down to the bullpen. "Mr. Steinecke says to hurry up and get ready," the batboy told Overby.

"What am I going to do?" Overby gasped to his warm-up catcher. "If Bill finds out I traded away the baseballs, he'll kill me."

"Don't worry about it, kid," replied the bullpen veteran, who over the years had learned all the tricks of the trade. "Just get up and pretend you're throwing to me. Steinecke can't see what's really going on way out here. And besides, the Sox aren't going to get any more runs anyway. Bill won't even need you."

On the bullpen mound, Overby went into his pitching motion—and threw the first invisible pitch of his pro career. The grinning catcher slapped his mitt and pretended to throw the imaginary ball back. Happy that the scheme was working, Overby continued to warm up without a ball. But the White Sox scored again to pull within a run of the Braves. Overby gulped, threw the invisible ball harder, and prayed that the game would end.

Instead, the White Sox rapped out another hit to tie the score at 11–11. With nobody out and the bases loaded, Steinecke signaled Overby to come in.

Overby figured that even though he hadn't thrown a real baseball all night, at least he would get some warm-up throws when he reached the mound. But the plate umpire had some bad news for him. "We're getting too close to curfew," said the ump. "You don't have time for any warm-ups."

Overby turned to Steinecke for help. "Bill, he can't do that to me, can he?"

"That's OK," replied the manager. "It looked like your fastball was working out there in the bullpen. It's a hot night. You should be plenty warmed up."

Moments later, Overby looked around at the three White Sox dancing off the bases and went into his stretch. Then he threw his first real pitch of the night— the change-up-knuckleball. The batter rapped a line drive, but it was caught by third baseman Ron Hunt who stepped on the bag for the second out as the runner on third took off with the crack of the bat. Hunt then saw that the runner on first was halfway to second, so the fielder fired the ball across the diamond and nipped the runner. It was a triple play!

To cap off the incredible night, the Braves scored in the bottom of the ninth to win the game. Amazingly, Dennis Overby, who had warmed up with an invisible ball, had won his first professional game on just one pitch!

Steinecke was so pleased with Overby's performance that he returned the rookie to the starting rotation. Overby went on to win eight more games and lead McCook to the Nebraska State League Championship, finishing the season with a 9–2 record and an ERA of under 2.00.

And he never threw another invisible pitch again.

11 ◆ PA'S PROMISE

Pro bowler Sandy Finkelstein wears a gold-and-diamond ring for bowling the only perfect 300 game of his life. It's proof that his dead grandfather had kept his promise.

When Sandy was 12 years old, his dad died, so his grandfather, Dominic Berardi, helped raise him. Over the years, the lonely youngster and the elderly man became very close. Sandy called his grandfather "Pa." And Berardi, who was born in Italy, affectionately called his grandson "Sanduce" (pronounced san-DO-che), which means little Sandy in Italian.

Sandy, who learned to bowl while growing up in Cortland, New York, dreamed of becoming a pro bowler. On a visit home from college, he confided his secret desire to Pa. Sandy was afraid his grandfather would scoff at his dream. Pa, who had worked hard to support nine children, never had time for things like bowling. But although the old man didn't know anything about the sport, he told his grandson, "Sanduce, if that will make you happy, then that's what you should do."

With Pa's encouragement and support, Sandy was more determined than ever to make the long, hard climb to the pros. He bowled whenever possible while still working his way through school at the University of Buffalo. After he graduated, Sandy returned to Cortland where he en-

tered every local tournament he could to gain experience.

By then, Pa was 80 years old and as excited as Sandy was about his chances of becoming a pro bowler. The two traveled together to lanes in Elmira, Ithaca, Syracuse, and Binghamton so Sandy could compete in tournaments. And on those long drives through the cold winter nights, their bond grew stronger than ever as they talked about bowling and about giving your best to whatever you do in life.

Often, at one of the tournaments, another bowler would ask Sandy, "Who's the old guy who's always with you?"

Sandy would grin proudly and reply, "Oh, he's my biggest fan. I don't go anywhere without him."

As they traveled from lane to lane, Pa improved his knowledge of the game while Sandy polished his bowling skills. Although Pa seldom picked up a bowling ball, he developed a keen eye for the fine points of the game. He didn't hesitate to tell Sandy how he could improve.

At home, following the bowling sessions, the pair spent hours discussing Sandy's latest game. "No, no, Sanduce," Pa would say. "You didn't pick up that spare because you were doing this." And then the old man would get up and pantomime the mistakes he had spotted in Sandy's approach or delivery.

Pa gave more than just moral support. During tough economic times when Sandy couldn't afford to enter a tournament, Pa often slipped him the money for the entry fee. "Here, Sanduce," he'd say. "Go sign up so we can go bowling." And the two would hit the road again to another tournament.

Finally, all that work, determination, and encouragement paid off. In 1972, Sandy joined the pro bowlers' tour and traveled all over the country, competing against the top bowlers in America. While trying to win tournaments, Sandy also hoped to throw a perfect game and earn one of the handsome gold-and-diamond-studded rings the American Bowling Congress (ABC) awards for a score of 300.

In February 1975, during a tournament in Denver, Sandy just missed rolling a perfect game. On his last ball, after 11 straight strikes, Sandy knocked down all but the eight-pin and finished with a score of 299.

At the time, when a pro bowler threw a 299, the ABC awarded him a gold-and-ruby ring. When Sandy received his ring, he proudly showed it to Pa and said, "I'm glad I got the ring, but I'm disappointed that I missed that 300. I'm afraid now that I'll never bowl one."

"Don't worry, Sanduce," Pa said. "You'll get that 300 game. I promise you."

One month later, Sandy's heart was crushed when his beloved Pa passed away at the age of 90. Sandy had lost his biggest fan and best friend.

At the funeral, Sandy stood beside the casket for one last look at Pa. Pat McEvoy, his boyhood chum and owner of the funeral home, waited while Sandy said good-bye to Pa. Suddenly, Sandy tugged the prized ring off his finger and handed it to McEvoy. "Here," said Sandy. "Put this on Pa."

McEvoy knew how much the ring meant to his friend. "Are you sure, Sandy?" he asked. "You know you'll never see it again."

Sandy nodded, blinking back the tears. "It's the most valuable thing I own. But I

want Pa to have it for all the things he did for me. He earned it as much as I did."

Two days after the funeral, Sandy flew to Sacramento, California, for a tournament. Still grieving over his loss, Sandy went straight from the airport to the bowling alley. He didn't feel much like bowling, but he was a professional and he knew he had to do his best. Pa would have wanted it that way.

When he was set to throw his first ball, Sandy suddenly felt that same warm, comfortable feeling he always had whenever Pa was in the crowd. Somehow he knew Pa was with him in spirit. The bowler rolled a strike . . . and another . . . and another. To his amazement, Sandy found himself in a perfect groove and was tossing nothing but strikes.

The seventh, eighth, and ninth frames were just like the previous six—all strikes. Now Sandy was faced with the pressure-packed tenth and final frame in which he needed three more strikes for that sought-after perfect game. The crowd behind him cheered when he rolled his tenth straight strike. The roar was even louder when he nailed the next strike, too.

One more strike and Sandy would have his 300 game. He could feel his body tense up. He took a deep breath and remembered Pa's words, "Don't worry, Sanduce. You'll get that 300 game. I promise you." All the pressure and doubts about making that last difficult strike vanished from Sandy's mind. He tossed his ball and watched all ten pins fall. Sandy had finally thrown his 300 game!

Instead of leaping and dancing for joy, Sandy dropped to his knees, raised his eyes, and silently said, "Thank you, Pa!"

Sandy would now have a new gold-and-diamond ring to replace the ring he had left with Pa.

As soon as he could pull himself away from the crowd of well-wishers, Sandy rushed to a telephone to relay the news of his perfect game to his mother. "You know, Mom," Sandy said tearfully. "It's just like Pa promised. He's still watching over me."

12 ◆ DUEL TO DARKNESS

On May 1, 1920, Brooklyn Dodgers hurler Leon Cadore and Boston Braves fireballer Joe Oeschger waged the greatest pitching duel in major-league history.

Relying on guts, determination, and a strong right arm, each man threw his best stuff—for an incredible 26 innings! That's almost the same as pitching a triple-header in one afternoon. The two veteran hurlers started and finished the longest big-league game on record, yet they wound up without a win or a loss. That's because the game ended in a 1–1 tie!

When Oeschger took the mound at Braves Field for the 3 p.m. contest, he was determined to settle an old score with Cadore. Earlier in the season, Cadore had beaten him 1–0 in 11 innings.

Brooklyn scored its only run of the day in the top of the fifth inning., Ernie Krueger walked, reached second on a ground-out, and scored on a base hit by Ivy Olson. Boston tied the score in the bottom of the sixth when Walt Cruise tripled and later scored on Tony Boeckel's single.

That was the last run either pitcher gave up in the contest.

However, Cadore almost lost the game in the bottom of the ninth when the Braves loaded the bases with one out. On the bench, Oeschger shouted encouragement to batter Charlie Pick. A fly ball, a slow grounder or a cheap hit would mean victory—and revenge—for Oeschger. But to the Boston hurler's dismay, Pick hit into an inning-ending double play. Oeschger slammed his glove to the dugout floor in disgust, picked it up, and headed out to the mound. He wondered how long it would take his team to score the one measly run he needed to win.

Cadore was thinking the same thing. All he wanted was one lone run. Both pitchers bore down, each waiting for the other to weaken. But neither caved in. For every shutout inning that Oeschger tossed, Cadore matched him.

When the game entered the 15th inning, Dodgers manager Wilbert Robinson asked Cadore, "Are you getting tired? Should I get someone else warmed up?"

"No, I'm fine," he replied. "I'm not goin' to let 'em score. Just get me a run."

It was easier said than done. Oeschger continued to mow down the Dodgers. But he ran into trouble in the 17th inning when Brooklyn loaded the bases with only one out. Rowdy Elliott then hit a hard smash back to Oeschger who threw to catcher Hank Gowdy for a forceout at the plate. Gowdy then threw wide to first baseman Walter Holke who knocked down the wild throw. Meanwhile, Ed Konetchy tried to score from second base, but he was gunned down at the plate.

That was the Dodgers' only extra-inning threat.

Back in the Braves' dugout, Gowdy told Oeschger, "Hang in there, Joe. Just pitch one more inning and we'll get you a run."

INNING	10	11	12	13	14	15	16	17	18	19	20
BRAVES	0	0	0	0	0	0	0	0	0	0	0
DODGERS	0	0	0	0	0	0	0	0		0	0

He said the same thing for the next three innings, then kept quiet when Boston failed to mount any kind of a rally.

As he warmed up to start the 20th inning, Oeschger thought about the marathon he had pitched the year before—almost to the day. While playing for the Philadelphia Phillies in a game against these same Dodgers, Oeschger pitched a 20-inning contest that ended in a 9–9 tie called by darkness. He thought he would never pitch that long in a game again. He was wrong.

Amazingly, both pitchers caught their second wind after the 20th inning. Although the strength in their arms was getting weaker the longer they pitched, the hurlers were actually throwing better than ever. In fact, neither gave up a hit in the final six innings.

With both pitchers still looking unbeatable, it seemed like the game would never end. But at 6:50 p.m., nearly four hours after the contest began, plate umpire Barry McCormick finally called a halt to the game. It was getting too dark for the batters to see.

Both pitchers headed for the clubhouse with sore arms, tired bodies, and mixed emotions. They had pitched longer than anyone in major-league history—and they had pitched stupendously. Oeschger had given up only 9 hits while Cadore had surrendered 15. Oeschger had held the Dodgers scoreless for 21 straight innings. Cadore had blanked the Braves for 20 straight frames. Yet despite having pitched one of the greatest games ever in the bigs, both pitchers came away with only a tie and not a victory.

The game took a physical toll on both players. The next morning, Cadore couldn't even lift his arm to comb his hair. Oeschger was so exhausted that he needed a week before he could pitch again.

The names of both pitchers still remain etched in the record books more than 70 years later. Since teams today rely so heavily on relief pitchers, the tremendous feat of Leon Cadore and Joe Oeschger will most likely never be challenged.

13 ◆ THE NIGHT DANNY HEATER LIT UP THE SCOREBOARD

On a snowy January night in 1960, Danny Heater, a shy, skinny basketball player from Burnsville (West Virginia) High carved his name in the record books when he scored an incredible 135 points in one game.

Danny's amazing performance set a national high school scoring record. No basketball player has ever had a better night than Danny Heater—not Larry Bird, not Michael Jordan, not even Wilt Chamberlain, whose 100 points is the most one player ever scored in an NBA game.

And yet it was a feat that Danny Heater never really wanted to accomplish. In fact, he had to be pushed by his coach and teammates to go for the scoring record.

Danny was a quiet boy who never wanted the spotlight. Raised in a loving but poverty-stricken household—the family had no car and his coal-miner father had no job—Danny discovered that basketball brought him great joy. When he wasn't in the gym practicing, Danny would shoot at an old peach basket nailed to the side of his house. Even in the winter when it was snowing, Danny would clear a patch and shoot baskets in his coat and four-buckle overshoes.

He was a super basketball player. By the time he was a senior, the 5-foot, 11-inch, 145-pound center had led the Burnsville Bruins to an impressive 35–3 record over the two previous seasons. He had the best shooting eye and the quick-est hands on the team. But Danny often refused to shoot because he was content to pass the ball to his teammates and let them make the baskets and get the glory.

It didn't really matter. Nobody outside of the area had ever heard of the Bruins or of Burnsville, a small town isolated in the coal-mining mountains of central West Virginia. Scouts from the major colleges seldom knew about talented kids who came from families so poor their only hope of going to college was on an athletic scholarship.

Burnsville High coach Jack Stalnaker wanted to help kids like Danny. He figured the best way to attract the attention of college scouts was if Danny could break the state's single game-scoring record of 74 points.

So before a home game against Widen High, the coach outlined his plan: The team would feed Danny the ball at every opportunity and let him score as many points as possible. "This is the only time in my coaching career that I've ever asked a team to do this," Stalnaker told his squad. "I will never ask you boys to do this again."

Danny was horrified. "Coach, no, no. Not me. Let somebody else do it, please," he pleaded. But his teammates voted him down. They wanted Danny to break the record.

Two and a half minutes into the game, the Bruins were behind 6–0 because

Danny refused to shoot. Stalnaker called time-out and let Danny's teammates talk him into going for the record. "Don't worry about what other people think," they urged him. "We'll get the ball to you. You just shoot it." With that push from his teammates, Danny went back out onto the court and started scoring.

Danny shot from inside and outside. He scored off his own rebounds. He led the Bruins on fast breaks and scored on easy lay-ups. He sank hook shots and made baskets off of steals.

During one astonishing stretch, Danny poured in eight straight points before Widen could even put the ball in play. Danny intercepted a Widen inbounds pass and shot it into the basket left-handed. Then he did the same thing right-handed. After Danny grabbed the third inbounds pass in a row and scored, a frustrated Widen guard handed the ball to a teammate and said, "Here, you try. I can't get it in."

The other guard couldn't either. Danny leaped high to grab the fourth straight inbounds pass and put it in the basket. That made eight points on four steals—and only four seconds had ticked off the clock!

While Danny was running up his amazing point total, the Widen five did everything they could to stop him. They tried freezing the ball to keep it out of his hot hands. Even when they double-teamed Danny, Widen still couldn't prevent the one-man blowout.

Finally, late in the third quarter, Danny scored his 75th point to break the old state record, sending the tiny gym rocking with thunderous cheers. Stalnaker then called a time-out and told the Bruins to go back to their regular team game. But Danny's teammates wanted to help him try for the national record of 120 points, so the coach let them.

By now, Danny was so tired he could hardly lift his arms to shoot. But in the final ten minutes of the game, Danny scorched the nets for an astonishing 60 points! When it was all over, Burnsville had destroyed Widen 173–43. Danny had hit 53 field goals and 29 of 41 free throws for a record-shattering 135 points. He also pulled down 32 rebounds and had seven assists.

The Guinness Book of World Records says Danny scored 135 points. But it really should be 139. The scorekeepers from the two schools had trouble keeping track of Danny's rapid-fire shooting and their score books didn't match up. So after the game, the Burnsville scorekeeper erased a pair of baskets from his score book to make the tallies match.

The amazing shooting spree made national headlines and brought college scouts to Burnsville just as Coach Stalnaker had hoped. But at the next game, when the scouts came, Danny was playing on a badly sprained ankle. He still scored 29 points, but limped throughout the contest. The disappointed scouts reported that the kid had a nice shot, but was too slow for college ball.

Danny never received any scholarship offers. With the help of a grant, he attended the University of Richmond. But he was so shy and homesick that he dropped out of college after only a few weeks and returned home.

He never played organized basketball again.

14 ◆ THE YUKON WONDERS

In the most amazing quest for a championship in hockey history, an amateur team from the wilds of Canada's Yukon Territory traveled by dogsled, boat, stagecoach, and train to fulfill a dream of playing for the sport's greatest prize—the Stanley Cup.

More than any game, the incredible journey undertaken by the Dawson City Klondikers revealed the true determination, stamina, and courage of the players. What they had to endure proved they were tougher than any hockey team ever.

At the turn of the century, the gold-rush town of Dawson City in the far northern reaches of the Yukon was a hotbed of fierce amateur hockey games. The town's top team, called the Klondikers, was made up of nine burly, rough players including gold prospectors, a teenage goalie, and a defenseman with a medical degree. After beating most every other team in the area, the Klondikers were looking for stiffer competition. "Why not play the best?" asked player Norm Watts. "Let's challenge the pros—the Silver Seven."

At the time, the Ottawa Silver Seven, Canada's top pro team, was the holder of the Stanley Cup and had successfully defended the cup against other teams seven times in three years. So in the winter of 1904, the Klondikers sent word they wanted to play Ottawa for the treasured cup. The Silver Seven accepted the challenge from the Yukon amateurs.

"We'll show 'em!" shouted Klondiker George Kennedy. "We're the toughest, roughest gang of skaters in all of North America. The cup will be ours soon."

However, the Klondikers had no money and no easy way to make the 4,800-mile trip to Ottawa (that's like going from Seattle to Miami to Boston). So the team sought out a financial backer. They found one in Colonel Joe Boyle, who recently had struck it rich with a gold mine.

Boyle shelled out $3,000 (a huge sum in those days) to outfit the men and pay for their long, difficult journey to Ottawa. On December 19, 1904, the Klondikers set out on the first leg of their rugged trip. With cheers from the townspeople who lined the route out of Dawson City, the hockey team marched off behind dog teams and sleds—in 20-below-zero weather. Their first destination was Skagway, 350 miles south, where they planned to catch a boat to Seattle.

Despite the bitter cold, fierce wind, and deep snow, the team covered 87 miles in two days. But on the third day, several Klondikers developed blisters on their feet. They had to remove their boots and wrap their feet in socks, cloth, and newspapers. Fighting frostbite and exhaustion, they trudged on, but at a much slower pace.

"We can't give up," player Dave Fairburn told his teammates. "Just think of this as training to make us even tougher than we are. We have some hockey games to play."

Grimacing in pain and numbed by cold, they finally staggered into Skagway two days later than they had planned only to face some bad news. They had missed their boat by a mere two hours. Five days later, they caught the next ship. The 1,400-mile sea voyage on choppy, icy waters along the Pacific coast left the hockey landlubbers seasick and weak.

But the team stuck it out. For pride. For a dream. For a chance to win the Stanley Cup. After reaching Seattle, the Klondikers took a rambling, cramped stagecoach 200 miles back north to Vancouver where they boarded a Canadian Pacific train for the 2,850-mile cross-country trip east to Ottawa.

For almost two weeks, the Klondikers rode the cramped, smoky, wood-burning train as it slowly chugged over the Canadian Rockies and across the plains. The boredom and inactivity onboard nearly drove the restless players crazy until Colonel Boyle came up with a partial solution. He arranged for the team to use the smoking car for workouts. However, there wasn't much room to exercise, so the only physical activity the players could do was skip rope.

Finally, on January 12, 1905, 24 days after they first set out on their quest for the Stanley Cup, the Klondikers arrived in Ottawa. Unfortunately, they were five days late. That meant the Yukon team had only one day to get ready for the first

of the best-of-three-games challenge.

"No matter what happens, men," said Colonel Boyle, "I'm proud of you—and so will every hockey fan who learns what you've been through."

When the Klondikers skated onto Dey's Gladstone Avenue Rink for the first game, the fans gave them a rousing ovation. The team looked sharp in new black-and-gold uniforms with white knickers and striped stockings—all paid for by Colonel Boyle.

Although they hardly had time to practice, the Klondikers put up a valiant fight. The amateurs played bruising, hard hockey and held the sport's first superstar, Ottawa's Frank McGee, to only one goal. But the well-rested, finely-tuned Silver Seven played like the professional champions they were. Ottawa pulled away in the final two periods to whip Dawson City 9–2 in a physically taxing game that left both sides hurting.

The long, weary trip had taken its toll on the Klondikers. They just couldn't recover quickly enough from the injuries they had suffered in the contest.

In the next game, McGee took it upon himself to clobber the upstarts from the Yukon. He riddled the net with an incredible 14 goals—to this day the most ever scored in a pro game—as the Silver Seven trounced the Klondikers 23–2.

Even though it was the worst defeat in the history of Stanley Cup play, the Dawson City amateurs held their heads high. "For what we had to go through, it was a victory for us just to make it here," said player Jim Johnston. "We may not be the best hockey players around, but we proved we are the toughest."

15 ◆ THE FRIENDLY RIVAL

Track star Jesse Owens stared in disbelief at the flag signaling that he had fouled in his long-jump attempt. It was his second miss, leaving the world-record holder only one more chance to qualify for the finals in the 1936 Olympics.

The distance was just 23 feet, 5½ inches. Owens' world-record jump earlier that year was much longer—26 feet, 8¼ inches. But in the Olympic preliminaries, he had failed twice at the shorter distance. One more miss and Owens would be eliminated from the long jump.

Then, just when things seemed darkest, help came from an unexpected source—his main competitor! He was Germany's Lutz Long, the only jumper in the field with a shot at beating Owens.

The dramatic meeting of the African-American and the German hero is one of the great untold stories of the 1936 Olympics held in Berlin, Germany. Back then, German dictator Adolf Hitler and his followers disliked blacks and believed that whites were superior. Hitler hoped the Berlin Games would prove that white athletes were better than nonwhites.

But Owens, a student from Ohio State, proved the madman wrong. Jesse stunned Hitler and his Nazi followers by winning four gold medals in the 1936 Olympics. But without Lutz Long's unselfish sportsmanship, Owens would never have won a gold medal for the long jump.

Jesse had entered the 200-meter race and the long jump even though both events were being held at about the same time. He started the day by running two qualifying heats for the 200-meter race. Still in his sweatsuit, Owens then jogged to the infield section where the long-jump competition was just getting underway.

Because he was late in arriving, Jesse was unaware that competitive jumping had already started. He took a practice run down the runway and half-heartedly leaped into the pit. To his shock, the officials in charge said he fouled and counted his warm-up jump as his first of three attempts to qualify.

Rattled by the officials' decision, and still winded from the 200-meter sprints he had just run, Owens tried too hard on his second attempt. He misjudged the takeoff spot—and fouled again! Jesse was now one jump away from being eliminated in his best event.

That's when a tall, blond German tapped Owens on the shoulder and introduced himself, in English, as Lutz Long—the German long jumper who had already qualified for the afternoon finals. The black son of sharecroppers and the white German athlete chatted for a few minutes. Long, who didn't believe in Hitler's absurd theories on white superiority, then offered to help Jesse.

"Something must be bothering you," Long told him. "You should be able to qualify with your eyes closed."

Owens explained that he hadn't known his first jump counted as a qualifying attempt and, in his eagerness to make up for the mistake, he overcompensated and missed his takeoff point on his second try.

"Since the distance you need to qualify isn't that difficult, make a mark about a foot before you reach the foul line," Long told Jesse. "Use that as your jump-off point. That way you won't foul."

Owens thanked his rival. Jesse then dug a mark with his foot in the grass next to the runway about a foot short of the foul line. Minutes later, he soared into his third and final jump—and qualified by more than two feet.

But the drama wasn't over.

That afternoon, the American and the German dueled in a classic Olympic showdown for the long-jump gold medal.

Owens' first jump set an Olympic record of 25 feet, 5½ inches. Then he bettered that mark with a leap of 25 feet, 10 inches. But Long responded to the challenge. On his next-to-last attempt, he thrilled thousands of fellow Germans in the huge stadium by matching Owens' record-setting jump.

Now it was Jesse's turn. The American champion answered with another record-smashing leap, this time 26 feet, 3¾ inches. Long needed a superhuman last effort. Trying to put everything into his jump, Long overran the board and fouled. Jesse Owens had won the gold medal!

Jesse still had another jump coming. He was so pumped up that he leaped 26 feet, 5¼ inches, breaking the Olympic record for the third time in three jumps.

With a scowling Adolf Hitler watching grimly from his box, the first person to throw his arms around Owens and congratulate him was Lutz Long.

Years later, Jesse recalled that moment when the two Olympic heroes stood arm in arm as friends: "You could melt down all the medals and cups I have and they wouldn't match the 24-carat friendship I felt for Lutz Long at that moment."

Long and Owens became good friends and wrote to each other even during World War II when Lutz was a lieutenant in the German army. In one battlefield letter to Jesse in 1943, Long wrote, "I hope we can always remain best of friends despite the differences between our countries." It was the last letter Owens ever received from Lutz. Just days after it was written, Jesse's good friend and track rival was killed in battle.

Jesse stayed in touch with Long's family, and several years after the war, he received a touching letter from Lutz's son, Peter, who was now 22 years old. In his letter, Peter said he was getting married. "Even though my father can't be here to be my best man, I know who he would want in his place. He would want someone that he and his entire family admired and respected. He would want you to take his place. And I do, too."

So Jesse Owens flew to the wedding in Germany and proudly stood at the side of the son of Lutz Long—a great friend and Olympic athlete who placed sportsmanship ahead of winning.

16 ◆ A GIFT FOR BECKY

Pitcher Debbie Doom turned in one of the most amazing performances ever seen in international softball competition when she led the U.S. women's team to the gold medal in the 1991 Pan American Games.

In her first two starts, Debbie pitched back-to-back perfect games! The fireballing right-hander faced 42 batters, struck out 35, and didn't allow a single runner to reach first base throughout both seven-inning games. It was the only time a pitcher had thrown back-to-back perfect games in women's international softball.

For Debbie, the stunning feat was a gift to her close friend and former teammate Becky Duffin. Becky died of cancer only months before she could fulfill her dream of pitching with Debbie in the Pan Am Games.

The two first met at the International Softball Federation world championships in Illinois in June 1990, when they were on the United States team. They had a lot in common. Both were 28-year-old amateur pitchers and considered among the best in the nation. Debbie, from El Monte, California, and Becky, from Jefferson City, Missouri, instantly formed a close friendship that extended beyond their admiration for each other's pitching skills.

At 6 feet, 2 inches tall, Debbie had the arm and the stride to hurl a blazing fastball at speeds up to 70 MPH. She also had large hands that allowed her to throw a sensational drop ball that few batters could hit. But her one weakness was the inability to throw a good change-up—a pitch that is delivered like a fastball but is much slower.

The change-up was Becky's specialty, and she used it to fool batters. With the pitch, Becky went the distance in winning the longest national championship game ever played—27 innings. Once, in a regional game that lasted 33 innings, she struck out an incredible 62 batters.

During the world championships, Debbie taught Becky how to throw the drop ball and Becky returned the favor by teaching Debbie the change-up. After sharing pitching secrets on the field, they also shared their dreams in long conversations after practice. They both were determined to make the team that would go to the Pan Am Games in 1991.

"That's always been my dream," Becky told Debbie. "And I'm going to be on the team—or die trying!" she laughed.

Becky was the star of the international games. She won three of the U.S. team's ten victories, leading it to the championship. But despite her outstanding pitching, Becky confided to Debbie that she tired easily and that her back often ached after a game.

Following the international games, the two new friends kept in touch with regular telephone calls and letters. But they would never see each other again.

Within months, life changed drastically for both hurlers. In August, while pitching in a tournament in California, Debbie was seriously injured when a line drive struck her in the face, shattering her left cheekbone. The injury required extensive reconstructive surgery. During her long period of recovery, Debbie received dozens of phone calls and cards of support from Becky.

Meanwhile, Becky was pitching with increased pain and fatigue. Doctors couldn't pinpoint the problem until it was too late. Around Thanksgiving of 1990, Becky learned the worst news of all—she had terminal cancer and there was nothing the doctors could do for her.

Becky shared her awful news with Debbie and the two cried together. They also talked about friendship and softball, and life and death. Mercilessly, the disease spread rapidly throughout Becky's body. By Christmas, the powerful young athlete, who just the summer before had been the picture of health, was dead.

Debbie was grief-stricken and depressed. Her good friend was gone and it looked like Debbie's playing days were over. She feared that with the long layoff caused by her injury, she wouldn't have time to get in shape for the Pan Am tryouts scheduled for June 1991.

But as Debbie slowly recovered from both her injury and her aching heart, she felt a renewed enthusiasm and confidence that she could make it to the games—with Becky's help. After all, it was Becky who taught Debbie the change-up that could give her the edge during tryouts.

Debbie began the long, slow process of conditioning and sharpening her pitching skills. She worked out day after day during the winter.

When she arrived for the tryouts in June, Debbie hadn't played competitively for nearly a year. But most of the 40 others trying out for the team were young college players in tip-top shape and fresh from a spring schedule of collegiate competition.

Shirley Topley, the U.S. team coach for the Pan Am Games, bluntly asked Debbie, "You know how tough these tryouts can be. Do you think you can handle it?"

"I'll make it," Debbie answered firmly. "I'm dedicating this to Becky."

With her fastball, drop ball, and new change-up, Debbie wowed the coaches and made the team. "I've never seen anyone more focused or intense than Debbie," Topley told her assistant coaches. "She'll do great in the games."

Debbie's pitching was so outstanding during tryouts that Topley picked her to start the first contest at the Pan Am Games in Havana, Cuba, on August 6, 1991, against the Netherlands Antilles. "I won't be pitching alone," Debbie told Topley. "Becky will be with me."

From the moment she hurled her first pitch, it was obvious that Debbie was on a mission. No batter could touch her blazing fastball or deadly drop ball. Whenever she got behind in the count to the batter, Debbie stepped off the mound, and thought to herself, *OK, Becky. Time for the change-up. Let's go get 'em!* The batter would look for the fastball, swing wildly at the baffling change-up, and strike out.

In the first contest (a 4–0 U.S. victory), Debbie was untouchable. She retired all 21 batters in a row—17 of them by strikeout—for a stunning perfect game.

Then, three days later, Debbie astounded everyone by firing another flawless no-hitter—this time against an even stronger team from Nicaragua. She fanned 18 of the 21 batters she faced, and won 8–0.

When the last batter struck out ending the game, the U.S. players and coaches dashed to the mound to congratulate Debbie, who only months before looked like she might never play again. Her teammates were in awe of her remarkable comeback—and her even more incredible perfection on the mound. Tears filled Debbie's eyes as she accepted their handshakes and good wishes.

Coach Topley threw her arms around Debbie and said, "You were unbelievable! I know you were thinking about Becky."

"She was the greatest pitcher in the world," Debbie said. "If she were still alive, she'd be here, too. But since she isn't, I had to win for both of us."

17 ◆ THE BENCH-WARMER WHO WON THE ROSE BOWL

Fourth-string quarterback Doyle Nave and fourth-string end Al Krueger had been warming the bench the whole year for the University of Southern California.

But in the biggest game of the season—the 1939 Rose Bowl—Nave and Krueger leaped off the bench in the final two minutes to lead the Trojans to a stunning upset over undefeated Duke University.

Incredibly, the two heroes never would have been put in the game if it hadn't been for a little fib told by a gutsy assistant coach.

With a 9–0 record, the Duke Blue Devils were the number one team in the country with a defense so awesome that it hadn't given up a single point during the entire season. Duke had outscored its opponents 114–0. USC, meanwhile, was the underdog, sporting an 8–2 record.

Doyle Nave spent most of the 1938 season riding the bench. With three quarterbacks ahead of him, Nave played only a few minutes during the Trojans' ten regular season games—not even enough time to earn a coveted football letter. Krueger also played little throughout the year.

Neither expected to play at all in the Rose Bowl game. In fact, Nave almost didn't suit up for the contest. The day before, he slipped in the shower room and hit his head on the concrete floor, causing a deep cut. It took several stitches to close the wound and the team trainer suggested Nave not bother getting in uni-

form. But, despite wearing a thick bandage on his head, Nave insisted on dressing out. After all, this was the Rose Bowl and he was going to be in uniform even if he didn't expect to play in the game.

And what a game it was! A huge overflow crowd of 91,000 screaming fans saw a classic defensive struggle. For three quarters, neither team could penetrate inside the other's 35-yard line. But in the fourth quarter of the scoreless standoff, the Blue Devils bulled to the Trojans' 15-yard line where the drive stalled. Kicking star Tony Ruffa then booted a field goal to give Duke a 3–0 lead. With their tough defense, it looked like those were the only points Duke needed. USC just couldn't muster any offense.

Up in the press box, the USC assistant coaches who had been phoning plays down to Coach Howard Jones decided they'd done all they could. With three minutes remaining in the game, they left for the sidelines. Staying behind was assistant freshman coach Joe Wilensky whose only job had been to man the telephone and relay the information from the assistants to Coach Jones down on the field.

Because he'd spent a lot of time with the subs during practice, Wilensky knew something the other coaches didn't—that Nave and Krueger made a great passing combination. He had noticed that while

the first-string and the top reserves worked out, Nave and Krueger often paired off by themselves. The two would practice passing and catching for hours until they got the timing of their pass patterns down perfectly.

Now, with time running out in the Rose Bowl, Wilensky knew the Trojans' only chance to win was by passing. The top three quarterbacks on the team were strong runners but weak passers. Nave, the fourth-string bench-warmer, had the best arm on the squad.

So Wilensky decided to tell a little white lie to Coach Jones. While the assistant coaches headed down to the field, Wilensky pretended to get instructions from them to relay to Jones who was still on the phone. "Yes, yes, I get it," said Wilensky, acting as though an assistant was giving him a play. "I'll tell Coach right away." He paused a moment and then said, "Coach, send in Nave and have him throw to Krueger." It seemed like a desperate move to Coach Jones, but he trusted his coaching staff.

With USC on Duke's 40-yard line and only two minutes left in the game, Coach Jones hollered, "Nave, get in there and throw the ball! Krueger, make sure you catch it!" The two stunned subs bolted off the bench. They didn't say much. Both knew what they had to do.

On first and ten, Nave called a play that the two had practiced over and over. Krueger ran down the left sideline and caught Nave's pass on the 26-yard line for a 14-yard gain and a first down before he was knocked out of bounds.

Back in the huddle, a grinning Krueger slapped Nave on the back and said, "Call it again. I can beat these guys." Moments later, Krueger caught Nave's toss for another ten yards to the Duke 16-yard line.

Hoping to catch Duke off balance, Nave flipped the ball to Krueger out in the flat, but the Blue Devils swarmed over the receiver for a two-yard loss. Now it was second and 12 on the Duke 18 with a minute left to play.

In the huddle, Nave pointed to Krueger, and said, "Get in the end zone and I'll get it to you." At the snap of the ball, Krueger dashed down the right sideline, crossed the goal line, faked out the Duke defender, and then headed across the end zone. Meanwhile, Nave avoided a furious pass rush and fired a bullet toward the left corner of the end zone. In full stride, Krueger caught the ball and then cradled it in his chest. Touchdown!

The crowd went wild and cheered themselves hoarse as the Trojan players leaped onto the backs of their two new heroes. Only 41 seconds remained and the scoreboard read USC 7, Duke 3.

Thanks to four straight passes from Nave to Krueger, who were both named the game's MVPs, USC had done what no other team could do that season—score against Duke. When the final gun sounded, Nave fought his way through the happy mob of Trojan fans and collapsed on a bench in the tumultuous USC locker room. Still in a daze, Nave wondered aloud, "Gee, do you suppose I'll get a letter now?"

"Son," shouted an assistant coach, hugging Nave around the neck, "you'll probably get the whole alphabet!"

18 ◆ THE OLYMPICS' FIRST CHAMPION

Nothing was going to stop James Connolly from competing in the first modern Olympics—not the fact that his college forced him to quit, that his life savings were stolen, or that his journey to Greece left him weary and weak.

Thanks to his fierce determination, Connolly overcame these hardships to win his event in the 1896 Games in Athens, Greece—becoming the first winner ever of the modern Olympics.

Connolly came from a poor Irish-American family in South Boston. His young life focused on work, school, and sports—especially track and field. He excelled in the triple jump, which back then was known as the hop, step, and jump.

He practiced long and hard and became the national champion in the hop, step, and jump. With the same dedication that he applied to track, Connolly worked at several jobs in an effort to earn money so that one day he could attend Harvard University, not far from his home. Finally, at the age of 27, Connolly had saved enough money and enrolled at Harvard.

In 1896, shortly after he began his college studies, the news arrived in Boston that the first modern Olympics would be held in Athens. It was the city where the Olympics began centuries ago and were last held in the year 369.

At first, the announcement stirred little interest in the United States. At Princeton University, Robert Garrett, the captain of the track and field team and an outstanding shot-putter, convinced three of his teammates to go to Athens with him to compete. They agreed when Garrett, the son of a wealthy family, offered to pay for his teammates' travel expenses. The university granted them six weeks off from their studies to attend the Olympics.

Elsewhere, the Boston Athletic Association easily raised the funds to send five of its top athletes, plus a team manager, to compete in the Games. One of the athletes was Arthur Blake, a superb distance runner and a junior at Harvard. A school dean gave Blake permission to miss a few weeks of classes so he could go to Athens.

When Connolly heard that Blake was going, he also applied for a special leave of absence. But to Connolly's astonishment, the same official who told Blake he could go refused Connolly's request. "You're only an undergraduate," the dean told the freshman. "If you leave now, you will have to quit—and you may not be allowed back in."

Connolly was outraged. "I'm a good enough jumper to beat anybody in the world," he declared. "I'm going to Athens to prove it. And if that means quitting Harvard, then I quit right now!"

Connolly stomped out of the office and withdrew from the bank the money he had saved for school. Even though it meant delaying his college education, he just couldn't pass up the opportunity to compete for the glory and honor of the United States in world competition. So he became the 11th and last man to join the U.S. Olympic team.

The American athletes left New York on March 20 aboard the German steamer *Fulda*. The long, 17-day journey sapped the strength of most of the athletes—especially Connolly. His wealthy teammates traveled first class in roomy, comfortable staterooms on the voyage. They dined on fabulous meals served by white-coated waiters.

But not Connolly. Because he had to pay his own way, he had to buy the cheapest ticket available. That meant being stuck far below deck in a dank, smelly cabin crammed with supplies and with barely enough room for a lumpy bunk. To make matters worse, he was seasick and seldom ate.

When the boat finally arrived in Naples, Italy, a stop-off on the way to Greece, an exhausted, undernourished Connolly staggered off the dock—and straight into trouble. As he wandered about the city in open-mouthed amazement at the sights, someone bumped into Connolly in a crowded marketplace. When Connolly reached for his wallet to pay for a small trinket, he discovered that his pocket had been picked. All his savings had been stolen!

"What will I do?" he cried to his teammates. "I can't make it to Athens without money."

Garrett, the wealthy Princetonian, patted his now-penniless friend on the shoulder. "Don't worry about it," Garrett said. "You can come along with us. We'll see that your room and board are covered."

The group then crossed Italy by train, the Adriatic Sea by boat, and part of Greece by another train to Athens.

Weary and out of shape after the 5,000-mile journey, Connolly planned to rest a few days and then work himself back into condition since the Games weren't scheduled to begin for 12 days. Or so he thought. But to his shock, he and his teammates discovered that the Greeks used a calendar different than the one used in the United States. According to the Greek calendar, it was nearly two weeks later than the Americans thought. Olympic competition would begin the very next day!

The next morning, Connolly dragged himself out of bed for the opening ceremonies. He and the other athletes had to stand in the sun for three hours waiting for the King of Greece to arrive to officially open the Games.

It was just Connolly's luck that the first scheduled event was the hop, step, and jump. "I don't know if I can manage even one jump," a worn-out Connolly whispered to team manager John Graham. "I'm exhausted."

Graham figured the athlete needed a pep talk and gave him one: "I've seen you make it this far, despite all the problems you had getting here. And I've seen you jump. There's no one here who can beat you. Just remember. You're representing all Americans now."

In the event, contestants had to take a running leap, land on the same foot they took off on, take one step with the other foot, and then make a big hop.

Two Greek athletes were the obvious favorites of the thousands of countrymen who crowded into the stadium. But Frenchman Alexandre Tuffere, who also lived in Athens, made the best jump of the day—a triple jump of 41 feet, 8 inches—before Connolly, who was the last to jump, had his chance.

When Tuffere's numbers were posted, Connolly smiled confidently and told Graham, "I've jumped farther than that in the streets of South Boston."

Connolly then walked to the edge of the runway and, in a bold gesture, tossed down his cap a yard beyond Tuffere's best effort. "Mark me there," Connolly announced to the astonished judges.

As he stood at the line preparing to jump, all the weariness from the long trip and all the sacrifices he had made were forgotten. In their place, the young athlete felt a rush of strength and confidence.

He raced down the runway, hopped high into the air, took a big step, and then made a giant leap that left the crowd gasping in amazement. His triple jump was measured at 44 feet, 11 3/4 inches—more than three feet beyond Tuffere's best ef-

fort. Connolly had even out-jumped his own cap marker!

Even though he had soundly beaten the Greek favorites, the 50,000 spectators in the stands rose to their feet and roared their approval with cries of "Nike! Nike!"

"What does that mean?" Connolly asked.

"It means victory," answered a beaming judge. "It means you are the champion."

Late that afternoon, with the sun setting on the vast stadium, the awards ceremony made it official. Connolly mounted the victory stand and was crowned with the winner's olive-branch wreath. He then was handed a silver medal, which, at the time, signified first place.

James Connolly had become the first Olympic champion to win in 15 centuries!

19 ◆ RAGS' FLIPPED-OUT VICTORY

Stock car driver Alan "Rags" Carter came from last place to win the 1952 Florida Stock Car Championship—but he did it the hard way.

Going into the backstretch, Rags' car tangled with one driven by Ed "Banjo" Matthews, his best friend and chief rival. Rags' car flipped over, yet incredibly, it skidded across the finish line first to take the checkered flag—upside down and backward!

The sensational finish astonished fans and the other drivers, especially when Rags climbed out of the wreckage and calmly walked away without a scratch and with the victory.

Both drivers had won their share of wild, slam-bang, fender-crunching spectacles. But nothing in racing history compared to Rags' amazing win at Miami's Opa Locka Speedway on January 16, 1952.

Rags pulled his 1934 Dodge two-door, with a big number 3 painted on the side, into the back row for the start of the 50-lap championship race. Then he glanced over at the car next to him. Banjo Matthews, the easygoing driver from North Carolina, grinned back at Rags from behind the wheel of his 1937 Ford Coupe.

The two racing buddies were starting in last place with 32 other cars in front of them, not because the two were poor drivers, but because they were so good. During the regular racing season, drivers earned points for winning races. When it came time for the championship event, the drivers with the fewest points started first to make the race more even.

"Keep outta my way, Rags," Banjo drawled. "I'm takin' it all tonight."

Rags revved up his engine and yelled back, "Not tonight, old buddy! That trophy is as good as mine already."

Rags was a fierce driver who never quit trying until his car fell apart on him. But against Banjo, Rags knew he had his work cut out. Banjo was a skilled racer whose daring driving style had earned him the nickname of "The Opa Locka Wild Man."

When the starter waved the green flag, all 34 cars roared off in a fast-paced traffic jam. As the race progressed, Banjo skillfully worked his way to the front of the pack. At the 25th lap, halfway through the race, Banjo moved into first place. Meanwhile, Rags was still bottled up in the middle of heavy traffic. But eventually, the slower cars fell behind and others dropped out with mechanical problems.

Now it was Rags' turn to shine. With the pedal to the metal, the old Guthrie Auto Repair Dodge number 3 began closing the gap on Banjo's H.C. Wilcox Ford number 28. Rags was passing cars right and left—sometimes going deep on the inside of a turn, and at other times going so high on the outside that his fenders scraped the wooden fence.

With five laps to go, Banjo was so excited about his chances of winning that he almost forgot about Rags and his gritty reputation for never quitting. But when Banjo checked his rearview mirror, he was stunned to find the grim-faced Rags in the number 3 Dodge bearing down on his back bumper. After breezing along for almost 45 laps, Banjo was suddenly in the race of his life with a driver as good as he was right on his tail.

Banjo swerved his Ford back and forth across the track to block Rags' Dodge from passing him. But Rags had learned a few tricks of the track himself. Each time Banjo moved to block him, Rags bumped the Ford's rear end—a not so gentle message to Banjo to get out of the way.

The two drivers blocked and bumped each other around the oval for the next three laps. The thrilling, bumper-to-bumper duel sent the crowd of racing fans into a screaming frenzy that nearly drowned out the roar of the stock cars.

With two laps to go, and Banjo stubbornly refusing to let his rival pass, Rags tried to get by him on the outside. After faking a move to the inside, Rags jerked to the outside and sped up alongside number 28. But Banjo recovered quickly enough to cut back and pin Rags' car against the wall before he could pass and take the lead.

With one lap to go, the two rivals tore around the track at full speed, side by side, door to door, wheel to wheel, with neither one giving an inch. The cars banged together, scraping paint and metal, into the final turn and headed for what looked like a dead heat.

By now, the leaders had lapped one of the slower cars in the race, an old yellow car that was poking along the inside lane right in front of Banjo's Ford. But Banjo wasn't known as the Opa Locka Wild Man for nothing. He clenched his teeth and moved toward the middle of the track with Rags on the outside. Still locked side by side, the two leaders squeezed by the slower car, but the track was too narrow to hold cars three abreast, especially with two of them racing at breakneck speed.

Rags' Dodge banged into the retaining wall, ripping away boards and timbers. Suddenly, the crowd screamed in horror. Only 75 yards from the finish line, the rear wheel of Rags' car caught one of the heavy railroad ties supporting the fence. The jolt threw his Dodge into a violent, twisting spin.

Whipping out of control, the Dodge

crashed into the side of Banjo's car, sending his Ford spinning off across the track and onto the infield. After battling from the back row, and leading most of the way, Banjo was now out of the race with the checkered flag only a few hundred feet away.

But, incredibly, Rags' car was still on the track. After striking Banjo's Ford, the Dodge slammed into the fence and bounced high in the air. As it went up, the car's front wheels embedded in the fence and the entire front axle was ripped from the car. The Dodge then flipped over in midair and landed back on the track, but on its roof and facing in the opposite direction.

However, because of its forward momentum, the wrecked car skidded down the track on its top in a shower of sparks, with the grinding screech of metal on asphalt.

The sturdy roll bar and seat belt kept Rags from being thrown clear. Holding on for dear life, he skidded across the finish line first—and became the only driver to win a championship race upside down and backward!

20 ◆ THE BLIND BOMBER

The eyes of college basketball player George Glamack were so bad that he couldn't see the rim of the basket. To him, the backboard was only a dim blur.

Yet, incredibly, Glamack became one of the top scorers in the history of the University of North Carolina. He also earned All-America and the school's College Player of the Year honors in 1940 and 1941.

Because of his poor eyesight and his amazingly accurate hook shots, George was dubbed "The Blind Bomber," a nickname he wore proudly.

In fact, the worse Glamack saw, the better he shot!

As a child, George suffered from poor eyesight, but he refused to tell anyone. He didn't want to wear glasses out of fear that kids would tease him. Despite his vision problems, George turned into a fine young athlete. But at the age of 14, Glamack was half-blinded from a football injury.

It happened during a sandlot game in his hometown of Allentown, Pennsylvania. George was stiff-armed when he tried to tackle a ball carrier and was accidentally poked in the left eye. At first, doctors thought he would be blind in that eye for life. But George's mother spent weeks attending to her injured son, changing the dressing on his damaged eye several times a day. His mom's tender loving care saved Glamack's eye, but he never fully recovered his sight. Combined with the poor vision in his other eye, George could not see clearly past a few feet.

Yet the husky, athletic teenager was determined to continue playing all sports.

Basketball was his first love. But when Glamack tried playing again after his eye healed, he couldn't see the basket and could barely make out the backboard. He lost confidence in his ability to shoot, and instead of becoming a starter on the high school team, he wound up on the bench.

George prayed every night for help in regaining his confidence. One day during a high school game, Glamack was sent in for mop-up duty in the last minute. A teammate passed the ball to George. On a lark, George tried a hook shot from 15 feet away even though he couldn't see the basket. Incredibly, his blind shot swished through the hoop! To George, his prayers had been answered. He knew then and there that despite his poor eyesight, he would one day be a basketball star.

So he developed his own "braille" system. He knew that the foul line, the lane, and other markings painted on the court were a fixed distance from the basket. Using the markings as guides, Glamack knew exactly where to shoot without ever looking at the basket. Since he didn't need to see the hoop, George spent hundreds of hours perfecting a shot that was almost impossible to guard against. He would turn his back to the basket and shoot deadly hook shots with either hand.

From then on, he was a dazzling shooter in high school. When he graduated, George had grown to 6 feet, 6 inches and weighed 200 pounds and was recruited by the Tar Heels of North Carolina. He turned into a high-scoring starter by his junior year with the help of teammate Bob Rose, a forward with exceptional passing abilities. The two used whistles to communicate. Whenever George heard a certain whistle, he would get in position at a certain spot on the court and wait for a pass from Rose. True to form, the Blind Bomber would turn his back to the basket and score with one of his sweeping hook shots. Because Glamack was so much taller than most players in those days, defenders were seldom able to stop his high-arching hook shots.

In his junior year, George averaged 20 points a game as the Tar Heels soared to a lofty 23–3 record, their best ever at the time. They placed second in the Southern Conference, but won the conference tournament championship. At the end of the season, Glamack collected his first unanimous All America award and was named the Helms Foundation's College Player of the Year.

The following season, the Blind Bomber resumed his blistering scoring pace. Against Clemson, the Bomber poured in 45 points to set a new conference mark and was on his way to breaking the then national single-game record of 50 points when he fouled out with 3 1/2 minutes left to play.

Later, in losing to Dartmouth 60–59 in the consolation game of the NCAA finals, Glamack scored 31 points, a single-game tournament record that stood for 11 years. In his final season as a collegiate player, Glamack again made every All-America team and repeated as Player of the Year.

Glamack's sensational shooting did more than help put North Carolina basketball on the map. He inspired millions of young people to overcome hardships and disabilities in order to reach their goals.

When his playing days were over, Glamack's number was retired, one of the few given that honor. Today, hanging in North Carolina's Smith Center Arena, his number 20 has been an inspiration to other great Tar Heel hoops stars such as Michael Jordan, James Worthy, and Bobby Jones.

21 ◆ WHAT PRICE VICTORY?

Ever since he was old enough to sail, Lawrence Lemieux dreamed of winning an Olympic medal.

At the 1988 Games in Seoul, South Korea, he had his chance. Racing off the coast in stormy seas in his one-man sailboat, Lemieux was in second place, gunning for the lead. Suddenly, he spotted a sailor draped over the hull of an overturned boat and another sailor bobbing in the water.

Lemieux knew that if he veered off course to help the sailors, there was no chance of finishing first in the race. But he didn't even hesitate. He sacrificed his lifelong dream of winning an Olympic medal to save the lives of two fellow competitors.

Until that dramatic rescue, Lemieux's mind was focused on earning a medal. He was one of dozens of Olympic sailors competing in a series of races in different classes of boats that day.

Struggling against dangerous waves and fierce winds, Lemieux, a native of Edmonton, Alberta, Canada, kept his 14-foot Finn-class boat on course.

Suddenly, out of the corner of his eye, Lemieux spotted a sailor desperately clinging to the hull of a capsized boat. Then he saw another sailor floundering in the water. The strong current and wind were pushing both men and their boat farther out to sea, far from any Olympic safety vessels that patrolled the course. The two helpless sailors were from Singapore and competing in the 470-class race that had started before Lemieux's Finn-class event.

The skipper, Shaw Ciew, was holding onto the hull of his boat for dear life. But he had cut his hand in the accident and was rapidly losing strength from loss of blood. Meanwhile, his crewman, Joseph Chan, had fallen overboard and was fighting to stay afloat—while drifting farther away from the boat.

Lemieux could have sailed on and hoped that a rescue boat would come along to pick up the men, but he knew their lives depended upon him.

At that moment, a terrifying memory from Lemieux's own childhood flashed before his eyes. As a five-year-old, he was already crazy about boats. One day, he jumped into a small sailboat and set out for the middle of Lake Wabamun by himself—without a life jacket. A gust of wind capsized the craft, throwing the boy into the cold water. Swallowing water and thrashing about, he was on the verge of drowning when he somehow managed to grab a rope from his boat and keep his head above water. Then he held on until one of his older brothers rescued him.

With the memory of his own near-drowning still in his mind, Lemieux made a bold attempt to save the sailors. At that moment, an Olympic medal didn't seem so very important. He turned his boat into the screaming wind and reversed his course, a highly dangerous maneuver.

Meanwhile, Chan was in danger of drowning. Despite the fact that he was wearing his life jacket, Chan was having trouble keeping his head above water because he was weighted down by his foul-weather gear. "Please help me," Chan gasped. "I can't last much longer."

"Grab onto my boat when I come past you," said Lemieux.

"I can't," cried Chan. "I hurt my back and I can't pull myself up into your boat."

With one hand on the tiller, Lemieux leaned over and grabbed the back of Chan's life jacket and tried to haul him aboard. Chan was halfway out of the water when the small boat—built to hold only one person—nearly capsized. There was no room in the cockpit, so Chan clutched the side of the boat.

"Just try to hold on until we get to your boat," Lemieux shouted to Chan.

Against all odds, Lemieux steered his overloaded, tilted boat through the crashing waves and reached the overturned boat. "You'll be safer on your hull than with me," he yelled at Chan. "If we all try to get in my boat, it will sink."

Chan scrambled onto the hull with his teammate, Ciew, who was about to slip into the water. But Lemieux tied up alongside the damaged craft and helped steady it so it wouldn't sink. After signaling for help, he stayed with the injured sailors until a patrol boat arrived.

Once the pair was safely aboard the rescue vessel, Lemieux set out to resume his race. But he'd fallen too far behind to catch up. He finished 21st out of a field of 33 racers. There would be no Olympic medal for Lemieux in 1988.

But his bravery and unselfishness did earn him an Olympic award. Lemieux was summoned to a special presentation by Juan Antonio Samaranch, the president of the International Olympic Committee. Samaranch praised Lemieux's heroism and gave him the Fair Play Award for the 1988 Olympic Games.

When Lemieux returned home, another meaningful ceremony awaited him. Members of the Northwood Presbyterian Church in Spokane, Washington, had a medal cast for him. As he stood on the platform with the gleaming medal draped around his neck, the Canadian national anthem was played.

Then a tearful Lemieux modestly thanked his American admirers. "You spend your whole lifetime trying to achieve a goal, and my goal was winning a gold medal," he told them. "I didn't win a gold medal, but I won something even more valuable—the love you've shown me here today."

22 ◆ THE SOCCER GAME THAT WOULDN'T END

Forward Meri-Jo Borzilleri knew the high school girls soccer game between her team, the Lake Placid Blue Bombers, and the Peru Central Indians would be a tough one. Both squads in upstate New York had the talent and determination to win the semifinal match of the state sectional championship tournament.

But no one knew how incredibly tough it would be. The contest turned into an exhausting marathon between two teams so evenly matched that after a 72-minute regulation game and 11 five-minute overtime periods, neither side had scored. So they went back the next day and started all over again with a new game. This time, they played to a 2–2 tie after regulation and battled through 13 more overtime periods still scoreless. Not until late in the 14th overtime when Meri-Jo booted the ball past the goalie was the winner finally decided.

Win or lose, the girls had made history. They had run, dribbled, blocked, and kicked for a tiring 269 minutes—that's the same as nearly four full games—in the longest high school soccer match on record in the United States.

The amazing game started late in the afternoon of October 25, 1978. Both teams played brilliant defense, seldom allowing the opponent to mount any kind of offensive threat. At the end of regulation, the contest was scoreless.

As a senior, Meri-Jo knew that if the Blue Bombers lost, her high school soccer career was over. She wasn't about to let that happen. But despite her efforts to slip free for a breakaway, the Indians blanketed Meri-Jo with a smothering defense throughout the overtime periods. Meanwhile, Meri-Jo and her Blue Bomber teammates were just as stingy on defense.

As the overtime periods mounted up, the girls became more tired and sluggish. Still, they fought on bravely until darkness set in. The game was called a draw and officials ruled the teams would have to play all over again the next day.

A worn-out Meri-Jo trudged straight to bed after the contest and slept late the next morning. She felt refreshed when the whistle blew for the start of the rematch.

Playing with renewed energy and a strong will, Meri-Jo used her dazzling footwork to score both her team's goals. But at the end of regulation play, the game was tied 2–2.

Lake Placid coach Larry McFadden and Peru coach Susan Sterrett met with officials to discuss the seemingly endless stalemate. At the time, there were no specific rules on what to do when tournament games ended in ties. There were no provisions for sudden-death kicks.

"There's gotta be a better way than this," said McFadden. "These kids are worn out."

"It can't be helped," shrugged the offi-

cial. "We have to settle this thing today."

The match was being played at Willsboro High, whose team was watching from the sidelines. They were waiting to see who they would face for the sectional championship (which Willsboro won) the following day.

McFadden returned to his side of the field and gathered his weary team around him. "I know you're all tired," he said. "But you can still beat them. Try to stay as fresh as possible, so when you feel you really need a breather come and tell me."

Just before the team took the field for the first overtime period, McFadden spoke to Meri-Jo, his star right-wing forward. "You've played hard," said the coach, "and if you want to sit down, it's OK."

Meri-Jo shook her head. "This is a special kind of game," she replied. "I want to be in there at the finish."

The game resumed—and the overtime periods rolled by one after the other with neither side able to gain an advantage and score the winning goal. Throughout the long afternoon, the exhausted girls dragged themselves from one end of the field to the other, probing for a chink in the other side's defense.

At the end of the 12th overtime, Meri-Jo staggered to the sideline. "I have to take myself out," she gasped to the coach. "I feel like I'm running underwater."

During the 13th overtime, while she rested on the bench catching her breath, Meri-Jo felt a hand on her shoulder. It was her dad, Bill Borzilleri. He had been teaching his daughter to play soccer since she was in sixth grade.

He leaned over and whispered in Meri-Jo's ear, "Just remember the basics. Just remember all the things you did last summer that got you here."

Meri-Jo thought back to all the work she'd put into soccer the previous summer. She spent hours in the park near her home running wind sprints to build up her

stamina. She also placed pine cones on the ground and practiced dribbling between them until she could do it in her sleep.

When the 13th overtime ended with the score still tied, Meri-Jo was refreshed and ready to play again. She grabbed teammate Erica Terwillegar, the Blue Bombers' usual scoring threat in the middle.

Meri-Jo knew that when Erica was moving the ball downfield, the defense usually collapsed around her. In practice, the two girls had worked together on a passing drill with Erica feeding Meri-Jo as she cut toward the middle from her wing position.

"Either you or I are going to end this thing right now," Meri-Jo told her teammate.

It took them most of the 14th extra period to get into scoring position. But when they did, Erica and Meri-Jo executed the play just like it was another practice drill.

The outlet pass from Erica was picture perfect. Meri-Jo took it on the roll and turned toward the goal. In her mind's eye, the defenders standing between her and the net were just like the pine cones in the park. Effortlessly, Meri-Jo dribbled and weaved her way through the defense. Then she aimed and kicked.

As she watched the flight of the ball, it looked to her like a slow-motion film. The ball started on a low path and then began a slight upward curve. It seemed to freeze the goalie for a split second before she recovered. The ball nicked the fingertips of the goalie's outstretched hands and sailed into the net.

Meri-Jo finally ended the marathon. The Blue Bombers had won!

By the time Meri-Jo raised her hands in victory, she was mobbed by her tearfully happy teammates who all fell in a heap on top of her. Even though she was being crushed, Meri-Jo didn't mind. Her team had won the longest high school soccer game ever played!

23 ◆ TWENTY-ONE SECONDS TO GLORY

One of the greatest achievements a player can make in a hockey game is a hat trick—scoring three goals. In one amazing game, Bill Mosienko, of the Chicago Black Hawks, scored a hat trick in just 21 seconds—the fastest ever in National Hockey League history.

What made the record so rewarding for the 31-year-old veteran player was that he did it against New York Rangers rookie goalie Lorne Anderson who had taunted Mosienko for being too old.

When the Black Hawks met the Rangers on New York's home ice in the final game of the 1951–52 season, Mosienko and Anderson both felt they had something to prove. "Mosie," who was completing his tenth year in the NHL, wanted to end the season on a high note to help earn a new contract.

Anderson, on the other hand, was just starting his career in the NHL. After spending most of the season riding the bench, he wanted to show the Rangers he had the talent to take over the starting job next season.

Neither dreamed that in less time than it takes to tell the story, the game would land both of them in the NHL record books—one as a hero, the other as the goat.

The game started badly for Anderson. With only 44 seconds gone in the first period, Chicago's Gus Bodnar got an assist from Mosienko right in front of the New York goal and slapped the puck past the rookie.

As he sprawled on the ice in a wild attempt to block the shot, Anderson looked up and saw Mosie grinning down at him. "What's so funny, old man?" growled Anderson.

"You are, rookie," laughed Mosienko as he skated away. "We'll be back."

And minutes later, Mosie was back with the puck, just like he promised. But Anderson was waiting and made a sensational one-handed grab of Mosienko's shot. Before the period ended, Anderson smothered another of Mosie's shots.

"How come you're not laughing now?" sneered Anderson.

Mosienko shrugged off the insult, and the first period ended with the Rangers ahead 3–2.

In the second period, the Rangers stayed hot with two more goals while Anderson blocked everything Chicago fired at him—including another blazing shot off Mosienko's stick that Anderson quickly slapped aside.

But while the youngster was growing more confident with his blocked shots, Mosienko was studying Anderson's moves in the net, looking for ways to outmaneuver the goalie. "I think I got this kid figured out," Mosie told his teammates before the start of the third period. "He looks like a sucker for a fake coming off the wing."

With six minutes, nine seconds gone in the final period and the Rangers leading 6–2, Mosie finally got the chance to test his theory.

During a face-off, Bodnar controlled the puck and passed it to Mosienko on the wing. Anderson saw him coming and set himself for another block. But this time, instead of taking a shot, Mosienko made a fake to his left. When Anderson moved to stop him, Mosie zipped to his right and fired the puck past the surprised goalie for a Chicago score.

The goal was Mosienko's 29th of the season. In those days, anything close to 30 goals was considered a good season, so Mosie retrieved the puck and handed it to his coach to save as a keepsake.

"Hold on to this for me," he told Coach Ebbie Goodfellow. "It may be the last one of the season for me."

The Rangers and the Black Hawks faced off again at center ice following Mosie's goal. Like before, Bodnar controlled the puck and passed it to Mosienko, who maneuvered around a Rangers' defenseman and skated toward Anderson. *If I can beat him once, I can do it again,* Mosie thought to himself. *He won't be expecting me to fake him out twice in a row.* Mosienko had read the rookie perfectly. Anderson, who was crouched in front of the net, took the fake for the second time. And when he was out of position, Mosie fired the puck into the right corner of the net for his 30th goal of the season.

The clock read 6:20—only 11 seconds had elapsed between the two goals.

When Mosienko grabbed the puck out of the net to save with his other one, Anderson grumbled, "Don't ever try that on me again."

"Don't worry," Mosie grinned. "I won't."

Again the teams gathered at center ice for another face-off. This time the puck went to Chicago's George Gee, who fed the puck to Mosienko on the right wing. Mosie then weaved his way through two New York defensemen and bore down on Anderson. *He's going to be ready for it this time,* Mosie reminded himself. Anderson was in a deep crouch in front of the goal, his arms outstretched. Mosie kept coming, but instead of trying a fake, he pulled up as if he was going to feed the puck to Gee coming in on the left wing. Anderson took a quick glance at Gee. In that split second, Mosie blasted the puck past Anderson's shoulder and into the top corner of the net.

The clock read 6:30. Incredibly, Mosienko had scored his hat trick in a blazing 21 seconds! But at first it didn't dawn on him what a historic feat it really was. After handing over the third puck for Coach Goodfellow to hold, Mosienko was puzzled by the crowd's reaction. "These are all Ranger fans," he told the coach. "Why are they cheering?"

"Don't you know?" Goodfellow said. "They're cheering for you! You just set a new record."

Mosienko's 21-second hat trick had shattered the previous record of 1 minute and 4 seconds set in 1938 by Carl Liscombe of the Detroit Red Wings.

Minutes later, when the final horn sounded and the Black Hawks had rallied to a 7–6 victory, Mosie picked up his three record-breaking pucks (which today are in the Hockey Hall of Fame). But before he left the ice, Mosie turned and looked back to the scene of his greatest triumph. Anderson was still in front of the net, hands on his hips and head down as if he couldn't believe what had happened to him. Anderson then looked up. For a moment, the two foes stared at each other from across the ice. Then, slowly, the defeated rookie goalie raised his stick . . . and saluted the veteran, Bill Mosienko.

24 ♦ THE DAY THE BATBOY PLAYED

Twelve-year-old Joe Reliford lived the dream of every Little Leaguer, every sandlot ballplayer, every kid who loves baseball. Joe pinch-hit and played the outfield in a professional baseball game—and set a record as the youngest pro ballplayer in the history of the national pastime.

In 1952, Joe was the batboy for the Fitzgerald Pioneers, a minor-league team in the Class D Georgia State League. He was a good-natured, eager-to-please youngster whom the players liked. In fact, the Pioneers often let Joe practice with them before games. He would shag fly balls and sneak into the batting cage where he'd take a few swings. Even though he was only 4 feet, 11 inches tall and weighed just 70 pounds, Joe could really hit the ball.

His favorite player was speedy second baseman Charlie Ridgeway, who often sat with the batboy on the team bus, talking baseball as they rode from town to town. In July, the president and manager of the Pioneers appointed Ridgeway to manage the team during road games.

Ridgeway had been the manager for a week when the Pioneers traveled to Statesboro to play the Pilots in a sold-out night game on July 19. To the joy of the fans, the Pilots began clobbering the Pioneers. By the eighth inning, Statesboro was slaughtering Fitzgerald 13–0.

Suddenly, a fan shouted to Ridgeway, "Hey, why don't you put in the batboy! Your players ain't doin' diddly!" Another fan chimed in, "Yeah, put in the batboy!" Soon the entire grandstand was chanting, "Put in the batboy! Put in the batboy!"

Ridgeway looked at Joe, who was beginning to feel nervous, and figured that since the game was a lost cause anyway, why not make a little history? So Ridgeway called time and talked with the umpire, Ed Kubick. "They're hollering for the batboy, Eddie," the manager said. "He's got a uniform and he can hit the ball. Is there anything in the rules that says I can't play him?"

"He's not eligible to play," said the ump. "But I don't see any harm in it. Just understand that if you win, you'll have to forfeit."

"That's not likely to happen," replied Ridgeway. He then went back to the dugout and told the batboy, "Joe, grab a bat and pinch-hit for [Ray] Nitchting."

Joe's mouth dropped open in shock. His stomach started turning somersaults and his knees began to shake. "You're not serious, are you?" stammered Joe. "I'm just a batboy."

"Well, they're hollerin' for a batboy, so we'll give 'em a batboy," Ridgeway said. "Now go get a stick and go up there."

Joe was so stunned he could barely move. Somehow he mustered the strength to find a bat and walk up to the plate as the crowd howled with glee.

Statesboro pitcher Curtis White shook his head in disbelief and asked the umpire if it was OK to pitch to the youngster. The umpire nodded yes.

The fans were on their feet, laughing and shouting at Joe. "C'mon, kid, hit it out of the park!" "Show those big bums on your team how to hit the ball!" "Let's see you club one!" "Don't be scared!"

But Joe was scared. He took some healthy practice swings and some deep breaths to calm his nerves. Then Joe got ready for the first pitch.

White, who was working on a two-hit shutout, wasn't about to go easy on the youngster. The hurler's first pitch to Joe was a fastball that blazed across the plate for a called strike. White cut loose with another fastball that sailed past Joe before he could even think about taking the bat off his shoulder. "Strike two!" shouted the umpire. The crowd booed the call and urged Joe to hang in there.

Joe stepped out of the batter's box and told himself to expect a fastball. He settled back in and waited for the next pitch. Sure enough, it was another fastball. But this time, Joe was ready and he smashed the ball hard down the third base line. The crowd rose to its feet, thinking he might get a double. But the third baseman made a great play by spearing the ball and throwing to first to get Joe out by a step. Even though he had grounded out, Joe received a standing ovation.

He received another big cheer when Ridgeway sent him to right field in the bottom of the eighth. Leadoff hitter Charlie Quimby then belted a pitch down the right-field line for an easy stand-up double. But Quimby decided to test Joe's arm, so he scampered toward third. Joe cleanly scooped up the ball and fired a perfect strike to the cutoff man, who nailed Quimby at third. Again, the crowd cheered for Joe.

But the youngster made an even more stunning play moments later. Batter Jim Schuster clubbed a deep fly that sent Joe dashing back as far as he could go. Then Joe jumped up, timing his leap perfectly. He caught the ball just before it would have sailed over the fence. Joe had just robbed Schuster of a home run!

The fans were so excited that they streamed out of the grandstand and onto the field where they shook Joe's hand and pounded his back. Even Schuster offered his congratulations. Others showed their appreciation by stuffing nickels, dimes, and quarters into Joe's pocket.

Although the Pioneers had lost 13–0, Joe was so happy he couldn't wipe the grin off his face for hours. In the clubhouse, one of the Pioneers told Ridgeway, "You better sign him to a contract, Skipper, before he gets away." Even though Joe never played in a real game again, he was forever proud of his one moment of fame. As Ridgeway told his team after the game, "Boys, you've just been part of history. Our team has the youngest player ever to play in a professional baseball game."

25 ♦ THE BOXER WHO REFUSED TO GIVE UP

No heavyweight boxer ever showed greater courage or determination than Joe Jeannette. In one of boxing's greatest fights, he was knocked down 27 times. Yet he simply refused to give up.

Only through sheer willpower did Jeannette battle back. Despite the pain and the fatigue, he bravely fought on against his opponent, Sam McVey. They punched, jabbed, and socked each other in an incredible 3 1/2-hour battle that lasted an exhausting 49 rounds—more than four times the typical 12-round championship bout.

The tough, iron-willed Jeannette finally won his astounding comeback victory when a weary McVey tumbled unconscious to the canvas before the start of the 50th round.

It was sweet revenge for Jeannette. In an earlier fight, McVey had won a 20-round decision that was unpopular with the fans. This time, to avoid any arguments over the decision, the rivals agreed to fight it out to the finish. The bout was staged April 17, 1909, in Paris, France.

Before the fight, McVey, who had won 13 straight fights, told Jeannette, "I intend to keep knocking you down until you can't get up again."

"You've got it wrong, Sam," replied Jeannette. "You're the one who's going down for the count!"

At the opening bell, McVey rushed across the ring and swarmed all over his surprised opponent with a flurry of lightning fast punches. Jeannette fell flat on his back before the crowd had time to sit down. Thinking Jeannette had been knocked out and the fight was over before it had barely started, the fans let out a howl of protest. The noise aroused Jeannette, and he staggered to his feet a split second before he would have been counted out.

But the quick knockdown was the first of many to follow. To the fans at ringside, McVey looked unbeatable. The 200-pound boxer, who weighed 15 pounds more than Jeannette, used his extra weight advantage and his superb boxing skills to knock Jeannette off his feet again and again. Twenty-one times in the first 19 rounds Jeannette was battered to the floor. But he couldn't be kept down.

Each time he hit the canvas, Jeannette shook his head and slowly climbed to his feet. Each time, the crowd expected him to stay down. And each time, Jeannette rose to his feet as the fans cheered his incredible courage.

In the 16th round, McVey connected with a powerful uppercut that sent Jeannette crashing to the canvas once again. The count reached eight when Jeannette was saved by the bell. McVey was convinced that he would win the fight with one more knockdown. But during the 17th round, Jeannette took every punch McVey threw and refused to give up.

When the bell sounded, Jeannette's handlers ran into the ring and guided their dazed fighter back to his corner.

"Give it up, Joe," pleaded handler Willie Lewis. "You already proved you can take it."

Jeannette could hardly hold his head up. "No," he snapped. "Nobody's gonna think I'm a quitter. You keep me in there."

In a desperate attempt to help Jeannette, Lewis grabbed a bucket of cold water and dumped it over his fighter's head. The water revived Jeannette who found the strength to keep going. "I'll fight until I'm carried out," he said.

In the other corner, McVey was rapidly tiring from all the punches he had thrown. "How does he do it?" McVey muttered to his handlers in amazement. "I keep knocking him down, but the man keeps getting back up!"

Incredibly, the longer the fight went on, the stronger Jeannette became. Meanwhile, McVey's punches were losing their force and his timing was off. For every punch McVey now missed, Jeannette was landing two or three in return.

By the 38th round, Jeanette had been floored an astonishing 27 times, and had yet to send McVey to the canvas. But in the 39th round, Jeannette connected with a powerful left to the jaw and for the first time in the long fight, McVey was knocked down. McVey got to his feet at the count of five. But the tide had turned.

Over the next ten rounds, McVey was decked 19 times! Between the two of them, their total of 46 knockdowns was a new world record. The crowd that had been cheering for Jeannette's unbelievable courage, now began to root for McVey's equally gritty refusal to quit.

In the 49th round, both boxers stood toe to toe in the center of the ring and pounded away at each other. But when the bell sounded to start the 50th round, it was all over. McVey staggered to his feet and fell flat on his face.

McVey was out cold after 3 1/2 hours of the greatest nonstop boxing ever seen. Joe Jeannette—the boxer who refused to give up—was declared the winner.

Jeannette then pushed his way through the mob of shouting fans who were pouring into the ring, and threw his arms around his dazed and battered foe, who had regained consciousness.

"We both won this one," Jeannette told McVey. "We showed them. Nobody can ever call us quitters!"

26 ♦ THE OLYMPICS' WACKIEST RUNNER

Long-distance runner Emil Zatopek wowed the sports world by winning three gold medals in the 1952 Olympics. Yet few fans know that he did it while joking and talking with his opponents—during his races!

And even fewer fans know that Zatopek unselfishly and unexpectedly gave away one of his cherished gold medals to the Olympic runner he admired most.

The skinny, 29-year-old Czechoslovakian army captain first made news in the 1948 Olympics when he won a gold medal in the 10,000-meter race and a silver for his second-place finish in the 5,000-meter race. Amazingly, Zatopek won with the most awkward running form ever seen in world-class track. He ran with his head rolling about, his arms waving, and his face grimacing as if in pain. Sportswriters poked fun at him, saying things like, "He runs like a man who has just been stabbed in the heart," or "He runs as if the track was electrified."

Zatopek took the ribbing with good-natured humor. He used to tell the press, "I'm not talented enough to run and smile at the same time."

Actually, the opposite was true, which he demonstrated in the 1952 Olympics in Helsinki, Finland. After winning the 10,000-meter race by setting an Olympic record, Emil entered the 5,000-meter race. To qualify for the event, he had to finish in the top five of his heat. Since he didn't have to win the qualifier, he decided to have a little fun during the race.

Zatopek, who could speak several languages, sprinted into the lead and then purposely fell back into the pack and chatted with the other runners. "Hurry up, or you'll miss the bus!" he told one slow competitor. "It's a lovely day for a run, don't you think?" he said to another runner.

Emil raced to the front again. But on the final lap, he slowed down and acted like a traffic cop, motioning for the Russian runner to pass him. Then Zatopek, pretending to be hitchhiking, hailed the Swedish runner. "Mind if I tag along?" Emil asked. He ran alongside the Swede before giving way and finishing third to qualify for the final race for a medal.

In the final, Zatopek was determined to win, but he still found time to talk with some of his competitors. He even advised the German runner to pace himself early and avoid wasting energy. But the German ignored him and paid the price by faltering on the final lap.

It was on the last turn that Zatopek thrilled the crowd. He was in fourth place when he made his move, swinging to an outside lane. Then, with an amazing sprint, he exploded past the front-runners and hit the tape first. In winning his second gold medal of the Helsinki Games, Emil had shattered the old Olympic mark by more than ten seconds.

Later that day, his wife Dana won a gold medal in the javelin throw. Making light of "competition" between husband and wife, Zatopek told reporters, "At present, the score of the contest in the Zatopek family is 2–1. This result is too close. To restore some prestige, I will try to improve on it—in the marathon race."

Everyone was stunned because Emil had never run the marathon (26 miles, 385 yards) in his life. "It's a long race, but that's no problem," he said. "I'll have a lot of people to talk to."

During the race, he ran alongside then world-record-holder Jim Peters of Great Britain, who was considered the favorite to win. Emil cracked some jokes but got little response from the unsmiling British runner. About a third of the way through the marathon, Zatopek asked him, "Aren't we running a little slow?" When Peters nodded, Emil stepped up the pace, and by the 20th mile the Czech was cruising ahead of the 52 other competitors.

Crossing the finish line nearly a half-

mile ahead of the second-place runner, Zatopek amazed everyone with a time of 2 hours, 23 minutes, and 3.2 seconds—a mark that broke the Olympic record by a whopping 6 minutes, 16 seconds! He had won his fourth Olympic gold medal, his third of the 1952 Games.

Emil was already signing autographs by the time the third-place runner finished. Zatopek greeted him with a slice of orange and then told the press, "The marathon is a boring race."

Zatopek's three long-distance-running victories in one Olympics—a feat that had never been accomplished before—inspired young Australian runner Ron Clarke. From 1956 to 1968, Clarke set 21 world records in long-distance running. And during that time, he and Emil became close friends. Zatopek often gave him training tips and encouragement, and even rooted for him to break his (Emil's) Olympic records.

Yet despite being the favorite in five events in the 1964 and 1968 Olympics, Clarke won only one bronze medal for a third-place finish in the 10,000-meter race in 1964.

After failing to win any medals in the 1968 Games, a crushed Clarke spent a week with Zatopek at his home in Prague. When it was time to leave, Zatopek handed Clarke a small, gift-wrapped package and asked him not to open it until he was on the plane.

Once he was winging his way back to Australia, Clarke unwrapped the little box and let out a gasp. It was one of the gleaming gold medals that Zatopek had won! With it was a note that read, "Dear Ron: You are the greatest runner ever and should have won an Olympic gold medal. I have four, and that is too much. I want you to have one of mine. Your dear friend, Emil."

27 ♦ THE PERFECT SUBSTITUTE

When Dave Hanson arrived at the New Frontier Lanes in Tacoma, Washington, he had no plans to bowl that night. He was there to work behind the front counter. But before his shift was over, Dave had made bowling history. He threw back-to-back perfect games—one of the sport's rarest feats.

What made his achievement even more incredible was that he did it as a substitute bowler in league play—while still doing his regular job of handing out shoes, making change, assigning lanes, and picking up loose pins.

On the night of December 23, 1991, Dave went to work behind the counter as the Bakery Drivers League was getting ready to bowl. But then co-worker Mike Muller told him, "The guys on the New Frontier Card Room team are short a bowler tonight. Can you substitute and help me keep an eye on things here at the desk at the same time?"

"I'll be glad to do it," said Dave. "You know me. I'll use any excuse I can to bowl."

Dave inherited his love for bowling from his father, Walter Hanson. For years, during his childhood, Dave and his dad bowled every Sunday after church. On Saturdays they watched bowling on television and studied the professional bowlers' techniques.

Walter Hanson often gave Dave tips: "Keep your approach slow and deliber-ate. And before you throw a ball, take a deep breath and relax. That's the secret. Just relax."

When Dave grew up, he became an ex-cellent bowler, averaging over 200 in var-ious amateur leagues. On this memorable night, he wanted to bowl well as a sub-stitute. But it was hard to concentrate on his game with all the distractions he had to deal with on his job. As soon as he took his turn, he would run back to the counter to help Mike Muller with the dozens of little chores it takes to keep a busy bowl-ing alley operating smoothly. Then he'd run back down to his lane and throw an-other ball.

Amazingly, despite dashing back and forth from the lane to the counter, Dave tossed ten strikes and rolled a terrific 278 in his first game.

In the second game, Dave couldn't miss. He nailed strike after strike. After the sixth frame, he scampered back to help out behind the counter and laugh-ingly told Muller, "Man, I'm really in a groove tonight! I've got my best shot working and everything is clicking!"

Muller abruptly turned his back and didn't reply. Dave wondered what was wrong with his buddy. It wasn't like him to act so unfriendly. But Muller was only following a common bowling superstition which says you never talk about a perfect game to a bowler while he's throwing one. Dave was so busy working the counter

between his turns bowling that he hadn't bothered to look at the score. As a result, he didn't realize he was working on a perfect game.

But word had spread through the lanes and bowlers drifted over from other games to watch him. By the tenth frame, Dave noticed that there was a crowd behind him and it had grown unnaturally quiet. That's when he glanced at the score—and his heart leaped into his throat. For the first time, Dave realized how close he was to a perfect game. He needed just three more strikes.

Suddenly, he recalled one of his dad's lessons. *Relax,* Dave told himself. *Just relax.* He stepped to the line and tossed a strike. Then another one. All he needed was one more. *Relax,* he said. *Just relax.* Like a guided missile, the ball headed right for the target and blasted all ten pins. He had done it! A perfect game!

But Dave's job shift wasn't over yet. So after all the handshaking and backslapping, he went back to work as if nothing had happened. And he still had one more game to bowl for the New Frontier Card Room team.

The third game was just like the second one—he couldn't miss. He'd throw a strike and then hustle off to help Muller at the counter or chase after a loose pin that had bounced out of another lane.

Some of the spectators that gathered around Dave's lane had seen a 300-game before. But no one there had ever seen a bowler toss *back-to-back* perfect games. Once again, people stopped talking to him. It was the old superstition at work again. But two perfect games in a row? *No way,* Dave told himself. *That couldn't happen to me.*

And in the seventh frame it looked like it wouldn't. Dave's ball scattered all the pins except the 10 pin. It wobbled but didn't fall at first. A gasp ran through the crowd and Dave sank to his knees in disappointment. But then another pin that had been spinning skidded over and knocked down the lone remaining pin!

Dave had no trouble striking in the eighth, ninth, and first two tosses in the tenth frame. By now every bowler in the building was jammed around his lane to watch history in the making. While he prepared to throw his final ball, Dave had to talk to himself because nobody else would. *Relax,* he reminded himself. *Take your time. Do just like Dad said.*

Dave went into his deliberate, slow-motion approach—and threw his 24th consecutive strike! He had done what few in bowling history had ever accomplished before—back-to-back perfect games!

Pandemonium erupted around the bowler. It took 20 minutes before the crowd thinned out and Dave made his way back to the front counter. Mike Muller gave him a bear hug and then, with a grin, handed Dave a broom. "Here you go, champ," said Muller. "Now you can go sweep up all the other lanes!"

28 ◆ 'WE'RE GOING TO WIN THIS ONE—FOR DAD'

When St. Louis Cardinals pitcher Mort Cooper and his brother, catcher Walker Cooper, took their positions in the second game of the 1943 World Series, their hearts were breaking.

Earlier in the day, Mort had received a call at his hotel from another brother, Sam, back home in Independence, Missouri. "Pop is dead," said a tearful Sam. "He passed away in the night."

For Mort and Walker, the tragic news was an unexpected, terrible blow. They knew their father, Robert Cooper, Sr., a mail carrier, had heart problems. But their dad was only 58 years old and appeared healthy before they left to face the Yankees in New York. He was making plans to be in St. Louis when the Cardinals returned home for Game Four to watch his sons play together in the World Series.

The Cooper brothers owed a lot to their dad who loved baseball and shared that feeling with his boys. When they were growing up in Atherton, Missouri, he was their first coach. Mr. Cooper showed Mort how to pitch and taught Walker how to catch.

As the talented brothers grew older, Mr. Cooper encouraged them to set their sights on the major leagues. At the age of 25, Mort, who was two years older than Walker, finally fulfilled his father's dream by pitching in his first game for the Cardinals in 1938. Walker joined his brother in the Cards' lineup two years later.

They made a great pitcher-catcher combination, known as a battery, during their four years together in St. Louis. With his brother behind the plate, Mort was a three-time 20-game winner for the Cards. He finished his career with a record of 128 wins against 75 losses. Walker, meanwhile, was an iron man behind the plate—playing in 1,489 games during his 18 years in the bigs while sporting a solid .285 lifetime batting average.

But the most difficult, heart-wrenching game the Cooper brothers ever played was on October 6, 1943.

After word of Mr. Cooper's death reached the brothers, St. Louis manager Billy Southworth called a team meeting. Mort, the Cardinals' best pitcher that year with 22 wins, was scheduled to start. The Yankees had won Game One of the World Series and Southworth badly needed his ace on the mound. But Southworth told the Coopers, "You have a tough decision to make. You don't have to play, of course."

Mort and Walker didn't even have to talk it over. They knew how proud their father was of them. "We'll play," Mort told Southworth. "Dad would have wanted us to."

When the Cooper brothers trotted out onto the field for Game Two, Mort turned to Walker and said, "We're going to win this one—for Dad."

The big right-hander fired his first pitch, a blazing fastball, for a strike. From then on, Walker knew his brother was going to pitch one of his best games ever. Mort was pumped with confidence, knowing his brother would call all the right pitches.

At the plate, Walker helped his team by bunting runner Stan Musial to second base in the fourth inning. Musial then scored on a single, the first of three Cardinal runs in the frame.

Meanwhile, Mort was mowing down the Yankees. Through eight innings, he was in complete command with a 4–1 lead, having given up only four singles. As the brothers headed onto the field for the bottom of the ninth inning, Walker told Mort, "Let's finish this for Dad."

But it was easier said than done. Mort had to face the heart of the Yankees' lineup. Leadoff batter Bill Johnson rapped a double, and then Charley Keller clubbed a run-scoring triple. Mort now was trying to protect a 4–2 lead with the tying run at the plate.

Southworth considered bringing in a relief pitcher, but when Mort glared into the Cardinals' dugout, the manager saw the look of determination on the pitcher's face and reconsidered. Mort got batter Bill Dickey to line out to second. He then coaxed Nick Etten into grounding out to second, although Keller scored New York's third run on the play.

Walker called time, trotted halfway out to the mound and said to his brother, "One more out, Mort, and we'll make Dad mighty proud."

Mort reared back and fired a fastball to batter Joe Gordon, who sent a twisting pop-up toward the Yankees' dugout. Walker flung off his mask, raced toward the dugout, and, just inches away from stumbling down the steps, made a spectacular one-handed, game-ending catch!

With tears welling up in their eyes, the brothers hugged each other. They didn't say a word. They didn't have to. For a few moments in the winners' locker room, the broken hearts of the Cooper brothers were given a jolt of joy for having won the big game for their father.

Unfortunately, the Yankees eventually won the World Series four games to one, just as the Cards had done to the Yankees the previous year.

Every game was a sellout, but there was one seat that remained empty during Game Four, the Cardinals' first home game of the Series. It was the one Mr. Cooper was looking forward to seeing. Before the contest, Walker Cooper went to the head usher at Sportsman's Park and insisted that no one sit in Seat 7, Row 3, Section 6. That was the seat the brothers had reserved for their dad.

Throughout the game, Walker carried the ticket to that seat in his pocket in memory of the brothers' number one fan.

29 ◆ THE JOCKEY WHO WAS AFRAID OF HORSES

Chris McCarron longed to be a big-time jockey just like his older brother, Gregg. Only one thing stopped him. He was scared to death of horses.

But the freckle-faced, redheaded teenager eventually overcame his fear . . . and then astounded the entire world of horse racing. Eleven months after riding in his first race, Chris broke the record for winning more races in a year than any other jockey before him.

The record-breaking race had special meaning for Chris. That's because the jockey he beat at the wire was none other than his big brother Gregg, who had inspired him to become a jockey in the first place!

Chris was a student at Christopher Columbus High School in 1970 when Gregg, who's five years older, started his jockey career at the Suffolk and Rockingham racetracks near the brothers' home in the Dorchester section of Boston.

The 5-foot, 3-inch, 95-pound Chris was fascinated by Gregg's exciting, glamourous life as a jockey. He started hanging around the tracks, doing odd jobs, tagging along after Gregg, and chatting with the jockeys.

In 1972, right after graduation, Chris got a job as a $90-a-week groom with trainer Odie Clelland. For months, Clelland wouldn't let the eager teen do much more than sweep out the stalls and walk the horses. The trainer wanted Chris to learn all he could about horses before he ever tried riding one.

When the day finally arrived, Chris, who had always been fearful of riding the huge thoroughbreds, hopped on a horse. He was nearly thrown off. Shaken, Chris jumped to the ground and waited weeks before he got up the nerve to climb on another horse. Confidence came slowly, but eventually he became comfortable riding the thoroughbreds.

Then came a historic event that convinced him to become a jockey. On December 6, 1973, Chris was at Laurel Race Track in Maryland when jockey Sandy Hawley rode home his 486th winner of the year. That victory broke the 20-year-old record for the most wins in one year set by the great Willie Shoemaker. (By the end of the year, Hawley had increased his total to 515 wins.) As Chris watched the record-breaking ride, he promised himself that someday he would be standing in the winner's circle himself.

With the encouragement and help of his brother and the trainer, Chris rode daily in early-morning workouts. Finally, the day came when he dressed in his silks and entered his first race. On January 24, 1974, 19-year-old Chris made his racing debut—and finished dead last! But just finding the courage to ride a horse in a real race was reason for him to keep trying.

Chris kept getting better and better

with every race. On February 9, just two weeks after his debut, Chris surprised his fellow jockeys by riding home his first winner. From then on, the victories began to pile up. Soon he was riding three winners a day, then six. By June, Chris was riding constantly—as many as eight races a day, seven days a week. (By the end of 1974, after being a jockey for less than a full year, Chris had ridden in an incredible 2,199 races—a new record.)

But as often as he won, one victory kept eluding Chris. He could never reach the finish line ahead of the one jockey he wanted to beat most of all—his brother Gregg. Chris had outridden most every other jockey, but he never won when the two brothers were in the same race.

As he started closing in on Sandy Hawley's record of 515 wins, Chris started having the same dream over and over again. In it, he saw himself breaking Hawley's record in a race in which he beat out his brother Gregg.

On December 6, 1974—exactly one year after Hawley rode home his 486th victory—Chris won his 486th race. Ten days later, Chris tied Hawley's mark of 515 victories.

The next day, racing fans gathered at the Laurel track, hoping to see Chris break the record. But in his first five races of the day—races in which his brother was riding—Chris failed to finish higher than third.

On the next to the last race of the day, Chris went to the starting gate atop Ohmylove, a bay colt and the favorite to

win. Gregg was on a long shot named Boston Ego. Chris wondered if he'd ever beat his brother and break the record.

Ohmylove broke cleanly out of the gate and immediately grabbed the lead. But on the backstretch, Boston Ego caught up with the front runner. Chris glanced at Gregg, who was riding almost stirrup to stirrup with him. It was just like in his dream. Chris saw how hard Gregg was trying to win, but the rookie jockey had a feeling that this time his dream was going to come true.

Chris pulled Ohmylove to the outside and urged his colt on. With Boston Ego now holding a slight lead, the thoroughbreds thundered side by side down the stretch. As they neared the wire, the two horses were still neck and neck. But with the skill of a veteran jockey, Chris edged Ohmylove into the lead and the horse crossed the finish line first, nosing out Boston Ego.

Chris had just ridden his 516th winner to set a new world record! His dream had come true! The happy teen was bursting with pride as he brought his mount to a trot. Just then, Gregg rode up and was the first to shake his hand.

Before the year was over, Chris added 30 more victories to his astonishing record as an apprentice jockey. His total of 546 winning rides in a single year was a record that remained unchallenged for the next 15 years.

The teenager who was once afraid of horses had made history in the sport of kings.

30 ♦ LIFESAVER OF THE LINKS

Professional golfer Mary Bea Porter kneeled beside the limp body of a four-year-old boy and realized she had been put in a desperate life-and-death situation. Trying hard to control her emotions, Mary Bea knew that if she didn't act quickly and calmly, the little boy would die.

Just minutes earlier, on that bright, sunny day of March 23, 1988, the only concern Mary Bea had was trying to qualify for the Standard Register Turquoise Classic at the Moon Valley Country Club in Phoenix, Arizona. Mary Bea—a member of the Ladies Professional Golf Association for 15 years—had just teed off on the 13th hole. The fairway was bordered by the backyards of big, beautiful houses where many residents were watching the lady golfers.

In the backyard of one of the houses was Jonathan Smucker, a four-year-old from Ronks, Pennsylvania, whose Amish family was visiting relatives. The Amish are a group of Christians who live a simple farm life and do not drive cars, watch television, or wear colorful clothes. Jonathan and his father, Christian, were watching the golfers when the boy wandered off and fell into a nearby swimming pool. With the heavy clothing Amish children traditionally wear, Jonathan quickly sank to the bottom of the pool. By the time Christian found his missing son, Jonathan

was limp and lifeless in the deep water.

Mary Bea was walking down the fairway, or links as golfers often call it, when she heard an anguished cry and saw the fully clothed Christian leap into a pool. The stunned golfer then watched as he pulled an unconscious Jonathan out of the water. Mary Bea then ran to offer help but was blocked by a seven-foot fence that separated the golf course from the pool.

The Pennsylvania farmer didn't know anything about CPR. In a panic, Christian held Jonathan by the ankles and began shaking him, desperately trying to get the unconscious boy breathing again.

Mary Bea was the only one close enough to help, but the tall, wrought iron fence prevented her from reaching the Smuckers. She shouted for her caddie, Wayne Sharpe, who picked up the 5-foot, 7-inch, 150-pound golfer and boosted her over the fence.

Christian handed his son to Mary Bea. "Please help me!" he cried. I don't know what to do. You've got to save my child!"

Mary Bea had not been trained in CPR either, but she knew the lifesaving technique from watching it being performed on television. Jonathan wasn't breathing, so she laid him on the ground and started puffing short breaths into his mouth. When Mary Bea looked into Jonathan's gray, lifeless face, she thought of her own five-year-old son, Joseph.

Somehow, some way, she knew she had to save this child's life. Fighting the urge to panic, Mary Bea continued giving Jonathan mouth-to-mouth resuscitation. Finally, to her great joy, she felt his chest heaving. She puffed more breaths into his mouth as the little boy began coughing and his eyes began fluttering.

Mary Bea leaned back. To her, it was like watching a newborn baby trying to open his eyes. Eventually, Jonathan coughed up some water and started crying. It was music to Mary Bea's ears. By then, paramedics had arrived and they rushed the boy to the hospital.

Emotionally and mentally wiped out, Mary Bea collapsed in a poolside chair and tried to collect her thoughts. When the excitement had passed, she decided to return to the golf course and continue her quest to qualify for the tournament.

But the experience had left her too shaken. Unable to concentrate on golf when she knew a child's life was at stake, Mary Bea shot poorly and finished with a terrible score of 76. She missed qualifying for the tournament by three strokes.

The next day, when her fellow pros learned why Mary Bea had failed to make the cut, 90 of them signed a petition. They urged LPGA commissioner John Laupheimer to grant Mary Bea an exemption so she could play in the tournament without having to qualify.

Laupheimer didn't even think twice. He said that saving Jonathan's life was a once-in-a-lifetime act of heroism that deserved an exception to pro golf's strict rules about qualifying. A grateful Mary Bea played in the tournament. But unfortunately, she didn't do very well and didn't win any money. However, she did receive something much more valuable—news that Jonathan had been released from the hospital and was feeling fine.

Later, the Metropolitan Golf Writers Association created an award in her honor—the Mary Bea Porter Award to be given to a golfer who performs a lifesaving act. The first winner was none other than Mary Bea herself.

After Jonathan returned home, his parents sent Mary Bea a thank you note and a picture of him. The photo showed a healthy, smiling and very alive little boy.

Now Mary Bea carries Jonathan's picture along with her own son's photo wherever she goes. "I'll always feel a bond with Jonathan," says Mary Bea. "It's like I have two boys now."

31 ◆ COLLEGE FOOTBALL'S TOUGHEST RECEIVER

Lehigh University senior Rich Clark made the most amazing play of his collegiate football career when he caught a game-winning touchdown pass against Dartmouth.

What made the catch so sensational was that Clark caught the ball with two broken hands!

In fact, the tough wide receiver from Tunkhannock, Pennsylvania, played *two* games with broken bones in both hands, refusing to quit despite terrible pain.

Throughout the 1991 season, the 5-foot, 10-inch, 180-pound Clark was one of the top receivers for the Lehigh Engineers. But no one really knew how much heart and determination Clark had until the second game of the season when the Engineers played the University of Connecticut.

By the end of the third quarter, Clark had made seven catches—including two for touchdowns. But early in the final period, he was knocked out of bounds after making another clutch reception. While he was sprawled on the ground, his left hand accidentally was stepped on by another player. Clark winced in pain and then ran over to the bench where team trainer Jack Foley taped the hand. "I think you'd better come out," Foley told the player. "This doesn't look very good."

Clark shook his head and said, "No, it'll be OK. I can still play." Before Foley could say another word, Clark dashed back onto the field. Despite his wrapped hand, he caught two more passes, giving him ten receptions for 117 yards in the game which Lehigh won 35–19.

The following day, X-rays revealed a fractured bone near Clark's left wrist. Although his hand was put in a cast and it was painful to play, he continued to practice. When the trainer suggested that Clark sit out the next game, the player told him flatly, "No way! I'm playing. I've still got one good hand."

But the very next Saturday, early in the game against Columbia, Clark suffered an almost identical injury—this time to his other hand. Clark caught a pass over the middle. But as he tried to pull the ball into his chest, a pair of defensive backs crashed into him and his right hand was caught between their helmets.

After the play, Clark trotted to the sideline in terrible pain as he held his rapidly swelling hand. "I hurt this hand, too," he told Foley.

"Now for sure you'll have to stay out the game," said the trainer.

"No way," Clark replied. "Fix me up. Then I'm going back in."

After getting his right hand wrapped, Clark played the rest of the game, catching seven passes for 120 yards to lead Lehigh to a 22–9 victory over Columbia.

However, after the contest, Clark discovered that his right hand was broken. When he showed up for practice on Monday, he was wearing a cast on each hand.

"Look, Rich," said Coach Hank Small. "I know how badly you want to play against Dartmouth next week, but a receiver isn't much use without his hands. How are you going to catch the ball?"

"I don't know, Coach," replied Clark. "But I'll figure out a way. Just give me a chance."

Clark worked hard all week in practice relearning how to catch passes without using his hands. Over and over, he practiced cradling the ball with his arms and body instead of grabbing the pass with his hands. At the same time, Clark had to learn how to block all over again. "You can't chuck [push] the defenders with your hands anymore," warned the coach.

"You've got to learn to block with your whole body instead of just your hands."

Every day that week, long after his teammates had headed for the showers, Clark remained on the practice field forcing himself to learn new ways of catching and blocking without using his hands.

The following Saturday, at Lehigh's first home game of the season, emotions were running high. The Engineers were hoping to extend their unbeaten streak to four games. Most of all, they wanted to avenge their loss to the Dartmouth Big Green the year before.

Wearing the two clumsy hand casts, Clark started the game, determined to show that he could still help his team. But in the first quarter, he dropped the only two passes thrown to him. From then on, the pass plays sent in by the coach went to the other receivers. Clark continued to block and run his pass routes, hoping that his number would be called again.

Late in the game, the Engineers trailed Dartmouth 28–23 when they mounted a last-ditch drive. Lehigh marched from its 20-yard line to the Big Green's 15 with less than four minutes left.

Coach Small then sent in a play that surprised everyone in the huddle—70 Pass Smash Delay. It called for Clark to delay a second at the line of scrimmage before cutting sharply across the middle. The play—Clark's favorite pass route— would challenge the heart of the Dartmouth secondary.

In the huddle, quarterback Glenn Kempa grinned at Clark. They had practiced the pass play endlessly. Both knew that by calling the play, Coach Small was showing he had faith in Clark's ability to make the catch despite his injured hands.

"This one's for you, buddy," Kempa told Clark, his roommate and best friend. "Let's get it done!"

At the line of scrimmage, Kempa barked out the signals. Clark took off on his route and cut to the middle at the four-yard line just as Kempa threw the pass. Clark leaped and cradled the ball softly against his chest and held on. When the receiver came down, a Dartmouth defender was already hanging on his back, but Clark stayed on his feet and lunged toward the goal line.

Clark then was hit by a second defender. But as he was going down, Clark reached out as far as he could. Holding the ball between his two broken hands, Clark stretched just far enough to place the pigskin over the goal line.

It took the officials a few seconds to untangle the players as Lehigh fans held their breath. Then the referee's arms shot up with the signal. Touchdown! Lehigh kicked the extra point and held on in the final minutes to win 30–28.

Along the sidelines, Clark's happy teammates pounded him on the back. Coach Small looked Clark in the eye and said, "I knew you could do it, Rich. Way to go. I'm proud of you."

Proving he could play with two broken hands, Clark caught eight passes for 141 yards the following week as Lehigh beat Northeastern University 35–22.

The casts came off two weeks later and Clark finished his collegiate career with 155 receptions—good for second place on Lehigh's all-time receiver list.

32 ♦ BOBO'S NO-NO

St. Louis Browns rookie pitcher Alva "Bobo" Holloman made baseball history the night of May 6, 1953, when he hurled a no-hitter in his very first major-league start.

Amazingly, his super debut—a 6–0 victory over the Philadelphia Athletics—turned out to be the only complete game Holloman ever pitched in the bigs!

Bobo was a superconfident, 27-year-old rookie right-hander who had played in the minor leagues for seven years without a single losing season. After posting a terrific 16–7 record for the Browns' farm team at Syracuse, Holloman joined St. Louis for the start of the 1953 season.

Despite his boasts about how good he was, the 6-foot, 2-inch, 207-pound hurler didn't impress his big league teammates. In four relief appearances, Holloman was tagged for five runs and ten hits in 5 1/3 innings for a whopping ERA of 8.49. In fact, he looked so bad on the mound that manager Marty Marion was thinking of shipping the rookie back to the minors.

Bobo never would have thrown his historic no-no, as major leaguers call no-hitters, if he hadn't pestered his manager every day for a chance to start. Even though rookies back then were supposed to be seen and not heard, Holloman asked his manager daily, "Are you going to start me today?"

And every day, Marion replied, "Rookies like you have to prove themselves in the bullpen before moving into the starting rotation. And you haven't proven yourself."

"But I'm a starter, not a relief pitcher," Bobo protested. "Now when are you going to start me? Today? Tomorrow?"

Marion shook his head and muttered, "You're driving me crazy."

"Either pitch me or release me," Bobo declared.

The fed-up manager finally gave in and told Bobo he could start against the A's in an upcoming night game at Sportsman's Park. Holloman jumped for joy. Now he would get his big chance to prove that he was a major league starter.

When Bobo walked to the mound that chilly night, only 2,400 fans were on hand. No one—not even the confident young hurler—expected to see a no-hitter.

Holloman had a few lucky breaks on his way to baseball history. In the second inning, Browns left fielder Jim Dyck robbed Philadelphia's Gus Zernial of a sure double with a running circus catch.

In the fifth inning, the rookie almost blew his own no-no when he tried to field Zernial's high chopper which was hit back to the mound. Bobo fielded the ball—but then couldn't get it out of his glove. When he finally shook the ball free, he dropped it as Zernial reached first. The official scorer ruled an error on the pitcher and the no-hitter remained intact.

Then in the eighth inning, A's batter Joe Astroth drilled a hard shot up the middle that looked like a sure base hit. But Browns shortstop Billy Hunter made a sensational diving play and threw Astroth out by an eyelash.

Other than those scares, Bobo mowed down the A's with an assortment of sinkers, change-ups, and curves. When he walked out to the mound for the start of the ninth inning, the fans were on their feet applauding. Holloman knew he was three outs away from a history-making no-hitter. The thought made his stomach churn with butterflies and his knees shake with nervousness.

Suddenly, Bobo, who had struck out two and walked two in the first eight innings, lost his control. He walked Elmer Valo and then Eddie Joost. With runners on first and second and no outs, the young hurler now faced the most dangerous hitter on the A's—Dave Philley, who sported an eye-popping batting average of .354.

Holloman bore down and threw his best pitch of the night—a sinker. Philley took a vicious swing and grounded into a second-to-short-to-first double play! The crowd stomped and cheered. Bobo was now only one out away from his no-no.

Holloman had never felt so much pressure. His heart was beating so hard that he thought it would burst. The sweating, anxious hurler pitched too carefully to the next batter, Loren Black, and walked him.

That brought to the plate Eddie Robinson, a slugger who was averaging more than 20 home runs a season. Bobo quickly got ahead of the batter with two strikes.

But on the next pitch, Robinson smashed a line drive down the first-base line, which was foul by just a few inches.

As Holloman and the nail-biting crowd breathed a sigh of relief, Browns catcher Les Moss scurried to the mound and told the pitcher, "I was this close to catching a no-hitter once before and I missed. I don't want to miss it again. So give this guy everything you've got."

Holloman threw a curveball and let out a happy yell when Robinson lofted a lazy fly ball caught by right fielder Vic Wertz. Bobo did it! The fans roared as the Browns swarmed around their new pitching hero. Bobo had accomplished what no major leaguer had ever done before in this century—pitched a no-hitter in his very first start!

After the game, the happy hurler told reporters, "This is the biggest thrill of my life!" For days, he was the toast of the town, posing for photos and signing autographs wherever he went.

His manager publicly apologized for doubting him. "I'm mighty happy Bobo pestered me into starting him," Marion admitted to the press. "He proved he's just about as good as he thinks he is."

But sadly, Bobo proved to be a shooting star rather than a shining star in the baseball galaxy. Despite a career that showed such great promise, Holloman started nine more games for the Browns that season and didn't complete a single one. He was sent back to the bullpen and finished the year with a poor 3–7 record and an ERA of 5.23.

Bobo Holloman never pitched in the majors again.

33 ◆ WHEN WINNING TOOK A BACKSEAT

Scott Bennett and Brad Howes grew up south of Salt Lake City in the fertile valley between the Jordan River and the towering Wasatch Mountains of Utah. The boys lived just far enough apart not to attend the same schools, but close enough to compete in the same leagues in baseball, football, and basketball.

No matter whose team won, Scott and Brad always shook hands and complimented each other on the way they played. The two didn't become close friends because they were always on opposite sides. But the boys grew up admiring each other's athletic skills.

And it was their childhood competition that forged a lasting friendship and set the stage for an extraordinary display of sportsmanship seldom seen in track and field.

It happened while the boys were members of school cross-country teams—Scott at Murray High and Brad at nearby Cottonwood High. During meets, as they pounded out mile after mile across the empty fields, Scott and Brad formed an unspoken bond. They learned to respect one another's competitive spirit and strengths. Brad liked to set a blistering pace early in the race, which wore down most other runners who tried to keep up with him. Scott, meanwhile, had a strong finishing kick, which had him breathing down the leader's neck on the final stretch.

Usually, the boys finished first and second when their schools competed. Sometimes Brad won; other times it was Scott who broke the tape first.

Their most memorable race—the one track and field coaches still talk about—occurred during the 1970 cross-country regional meet, with the winner going to the state finals. The event, held as part of Cottonwood High's homecoming festivities, was run during halftime of the football game between Cottonwood and Murray. Since the schools were only about ten miles apart, the stands were jammed with rooters from both sides.

At halftime, Murray was leading by two touchdowns and threatening to spoil Cottonwood's homecoming. So when Scott and Brad took their places at the starting line, each knew there was a lot more at stake than just a race. Brad felt that by winning he could salvage some of Cottonwood's pride at homecoming. Scott wanted to win to prove that Murray was the best at everything.

There were three other runners in the race, but all eyes were on Scott and Brad when the starter's gun went off. The group circled the track that ringed the football field and headed out the exit for the 2.6-mile cross-country run.

As expected, Brad quickly took the lead in a race that went through the rolling, grassy hills of Sugarhouse Park bordering the school grounds. At the halfway point, Brad had pulled ahead of Scott by nearly 300 yards while the other runners had fallen out of contention.

Despite the gap, Scott wasn't worried. In past races, Brad usually grabbed the lead, but Scott, with his strong finish, often caught Brad on the final stretch. Sticking to his race strategy, Scott steadily gained on Brad. By the time the two reached the stadium, Scott was only a couple of steps behind.

When the pair dashed through the stadium tunnel and onto the track for the final lap, the capacity crowd rose to its feet to cheer the runners who were now racing stride for stride.

But coming around the final turn, Scott cut to the inside to pass Brad and get in position for a sprint down the stretch. Just then, Brad also moved inside and the runners' legs tangled. Both stumbled. Scott managed to keep his feet, but Brad sprawled headfirst onto the track.

Scott ran a few more paces. But suddenly, he became aware of an eerie silence. The crowd that had been shouting moments before fell deathly silent when

92

Brad tripped and hit the ground. So Scott stopped and looked back at his lifelong rival. Brad, whose knees and hands were scraped and bleeding from falling on the cinders, was struggling to regain his feet.

Who won or lost the race no longer mattered to Scott. His friend and competitor was hurt. Scott knew what he had to do— he went back to help. "Give me your hand, Brad," said Scott. "Let me help you."

Brad looked up at Scott, smiled, and said, "Man, you're something else." Scott pulled his injured rival to his feet but Brad was hurting so badly that he couldn't run very well. So Scott put his arm around Brad and the two began trotting down the final stretch. The thousands of fans in the stands gasped when they saw Scott's gallant gesture and then erupted into thunderous applause.

Shocked by the unexpected spill, the track judges had dropped the tape that marked the finish line. "Get that tape back up!" a coach yelled. "They're coming in . . . together!"

With Brad limping the final 50 yards, and Scott helping him every step of the way, the two competitors crossed the finish line arm in arm. The coaches and the track judges then huddled over what to do about the incredibly unselfish act of sportsmanship they had just witnessed.

"One of the runners has to win, but that doesn't mean the other one has to lose," said Scott's coach, Sam Moore. "I know Scott wouldn't want to have his victory tainted. I say we give both kids first place."

Moore's suggestion won unanimous approval from Brad's coach and the judges. The race was declared a dead heat.

"I have never seen such sportsmanship," said Moore. "I doubt if I ever will again."

34 ◆ THE GIRL WHO MANAGED THE DODGERS

Ever since she was a little girl, Jill Baer loved baseball. She went to New York Mets games, studied box scores, read sports magazines, and discussed strategy with her dad. As a teenager, she had a dream that seemed impossible to fulfill—she wanted to manage a major-league team.

Incredibly, at the age of 23, Jill lived out her dream. She actually got to manage the Los Angeles Dodgers!

In 1978, Jill was a TV production assistant in Los Angeles when she bumped into Dodgers manager Tommy Lasorda and first baseman Steve Garvey who were guests on a game show in the studio where she worked. Jill realized that this was the moment that could make her dream come true. But she had to act now.

With her voice quivering and her knees shaking, Jill introduced herself to the two Dodgers, who were so friendly that soon she was talking baseball with them. Lasorda even quizzed her on her knowledge of baseball strategy and was impressed with her answers.

"How do you know so much about baseball?" he asked her.

"I'm after your job," Jill said with a sweet smile.

Lasorda looked her in the eyes and said, "Well, it's pretty hard for a girl to manage. You need lots of experience as a player or coach. And the players can be pretty hard to manage."

"I think I can do it," Jill said boldly. Then, taking a deep breath, she asked Lasorda, "Would you let me manage the Dodgers . . . for one day . . . in a spring training game?"

Lasorda laughed—until he realized that Jill was dead serious. To her great joy, he promised to talk it over with team Vice President Fred Claire. A week later, Claire called Jill and said, "We'll need your measurements for a uniform. You're going to be our manager for a day."

Jill couldn't believe it. Her fantasy was about to come true! A week before her debut as a manager, Jill flew to the Dodgers' spring training camp in Vero Beach, Florida. She was issued a new uniform—number 2, the same as Lasorda's. But it was so big on her 5-foot, 5-inch frame that it had to be altered.

When Jill was introduced to the players, most greeted her good-naturedly. But not all. Some thought her presence was a bad joke. She tried to ignore them. Over the next few days during practice, Jill took dozens of notes about the strengths and weaknesses of each player and she talked with the coaches to get some inside tips.

Finally, her big day arrived. With her uniform fitting smartly and her Dodgers cap sitting atop her curly auburn hair, Jill proudly stepped into the dugout to manage her first and only game.

Jill made out the lineup, which was the

same one Lasorda had planned to use in the regular season—except for one change. She switched Ron Cey from fourth to fifth in the batting order and made Garvey the cleanup hitter.

In the first inning, when the third batter went up to the plate, Cey, who had batted cleanup most of the previous year, headed for the on-deck circle. But Jill called him back and said, "You're batting fifth today."

Cey, who wasn't too thrilled with Jill's presence in the dugout anyway, snapped, "I bat cleanup."

Without batting an eye, Jill snapped back, "Not on my ball club."

The other players and Lasorda burst out laughing. Outfielder Dusty Baker, calling Cey by his nickname, shouted, "You better sit down, Penguin, or she'll have you in Albuquerque [home of the Dodgers' farm team] by the end of the week."

With a disgusted look, Cey shook his head and sat down as Garvey moved out to the on-deck circle.

"You know," Lasorda told Jill. "You're going to do fine. I'm going to watch the rest of the game from the stands." Then he left the dugout, leaving Jill to manage by herself. From then on, she had no more problems with the players. And when it came to strategy, she batted 1.000. She called for a hit-and-run that worked and a steal that was safely executed. What worked the best was the lineup switch. Garvey and Cey each collected two hits, and one of Cey's singles drove in Garvey.

Jill was having a great time managing until the seventh inning when she learned a hard lesson—you can't win an argument with an umpire. When an opposing team's runner on second base raced home, Jill noticed that he failed to touch third base. So she ordered her team to appeal the play. But the umpire ruled that the runner had touched the bag.

Jill raced out of the dugout and protested. Pointing to a footprint a few inches from the base, she said, "See, he missed the base."

The umpire, deciding to have a little fun at Jill's expense, kicked dirt over the footprint and replied, "I don't see anything."

"What are you doing?" Jill gasped.

"Some grounds keeping," the ump answered. "Now go sit down. The runner is safe."

Jill was so upset she threw her hat down. The umpire responded by giving her the thumb. "Go to the showers!" he thundered.

"I can't," she replied. "I'm a girl." Then she stalked off the field to a standing ovation from the players in the dugout and the fans in the stands. Jill may have left the game early, but she walked out a winner. Her team won 5–2.

She was happy, especially when Lasorda told her she did a great job of managing. Replied Jill, "All I can say besides thank you is that you should bat Garvey cleanup and put Cey fifth."

Lasorda ignored Jill's advice and batted Cey in the fourth spot as he had in the previous year. But in August, when the second-place Dodgers met the first-place San Francisco Giants in a crucial series, he switched Cey and Garvey in the batting order, just as Jill had suggested. The Dodgers whipped the Giants and went on to capture the National League pennant.

Jill was right all along.